Dear reader,

Thank you for allowing me to join you on your journey to greatness. Together we will discover your pathway to Freedom, Joy, and Abundance.

I think of you like a sister (or brother, you are welcome here too), and believe that it is my own personal mission to offer a hand back to those a few steps behind me on this journey we call life. I do that just as those ahead of me have reached back and given me a hand up.

You will find some clear advice within these pages, some personal stories from my own life, and you will take a peek into my own triumphs and failures. It is important on any journey of self discovery that we be absolutely honest with each other! While I am certainly not perfect (and never have been), I have reached a wonderful plateau; it's a place from which I can look around and recognize the wonderment of the universe.

Welcome to my world of Freedom, Joy, and Abundance, and may God bless you as you embark on a wonderful journey of forgiveness, acceptance, honesty, and discovery.

Here's to you!

First step: check!

All the best, Naomi

Please visit www.embracethemirror.com for more information, or to contact me personally.

Contents

Chapter 1
What is the Common Denominator in Your Life?

(Hint: The solution is in the mirror.)

No, I promise, there is no math involved. This is not a math problem. It's a "who are you?" problem. So...if it's not math, what does it mean to discover the common denominator *in your own life*? Continue reading this chapter to discover three steps to solving the equation.

You know, even though I was no good at math, I do remember having to solve many problems where I was asked to find the common denominator. All the years I spent looking for common denominators in math, gave me no clue that one day I would have to figure out who or what was the common denominator in my own life. Here's an example.

It was Christmas Eve, 2001, and at three o'clock in the morning I woke up in a cold sweat. My heart was hammering—pounding so hard I got scared that it would jump out of my chest. I felt the surge of panic like a cluster of spark plugs firing up in my belly. Tension spread from my core to my face, and down my arms. My breathing became rapid and shallow and I realized I was panting like a dog after a long run. And an elephant had somehow sat on my chest. The feeling was awful; I had never experienced such a terrible feeling of dread. Was I going to die?

A trip to the hospital's emergency room that Christmas Eve revealed that I was suffering from an anxiety and panic attack disorder. All the little signs and warnings that my body had been giving me had been studiously ignored; I had no time for such "nonsense" I thought. I was too busy to be sick. Isn't that what we all think? Women, whether they are busy mothers or pressured CEO's, are on the front lines and our battle cry is: "No time to say 'hello' or 'goodbye,' I'm late, I'm late, I'm late."

Now there I was hooked up to monitors. Denial was out of the window. I thought back to reflect on what exactly happened to bring me to the ER that fateful morning. The evening before the panic attack I had separated from my husband of only three months. At a time when I should have been blissful and enjoying my honeymoon and favorite time of the year (the holidays), I was going through one of the most difficult moments of my life.

My husband had taken everything I owned, packed it all up in a U-Haul rental truck, and driven to Texas. He left me in an empty house without even a cup to drink from. After he left I was so heart broken that I spent several hours curled up on the floor in a fetal position, crying my heart out. I was heartbroken, sad, ashamed, and embarrassed at my inability to pick the right man. I knew I was smart, but yet I kept dating men who were exactly like my father. I kept repeating history, doing the damn thing, and expecting a different result. No one had ever told me that I was the common denominator in all of my distress. Every twist and turn always came back to me. Every scenario featured… guess who? Me!

That next morning, I woke up to the harsh reality that I may turn fifty and never find someone to share my life with. I woke up to the reality that every single relationship in my life was a mess. My life was a disaster. I was bankrupt, over weight, and alone. In that moment, I realized no one was coming to rescue me and that it was up to me to clean up my act. Before this great awakening, I had – probably just like you - spent most of my teen-age years and young adulthood searching for 'happiness'. I never actually took the time to define 'happiness' figuring I'd know it when I saw it.

So, I kept looking for love in all the wrong places. I looked to be loved by people who were incapable of loving me, including my own family. I got romantically involved with men who were as broken as I was. Tip: Two broken vases put together do not make one vase that will hold water!

For whatever reason, I believed my family, friends, romantic partnership, or even the career I chose would and could bring me a life of joy, freedom, and abundance. I was like Indiana Jones looking at the chasm between where I was and where I wanted to go.

Lying in that hospital bed, I felt like I was standing at the bottom of the mountain, looking straight up at the daunting climb ahead. I had no clue how I was going to climb that mountain and the many other mountains I knew were ahead in my life. But the good news is that *I climbed them* and so can you. So…What's it like for me now that I've climbed my own Mt. Everest? I can honestly tell you that today I'm beyond happy. Joy has become a natural state of being for me. I feel amazing and blessed to have climbed out of the ruble and scaled the face of that mountain. I reached the pinnacle. I feel happy that I'm in control of every aspect of my life. Would you like to join me up here?

I can assure that no one is in control of my happiness; not my friends, parents, relatives, and not even my wonderful partner in life. I no longer look outside of myself for the things I desire. Instead, I look within. I now live my life on purpose and with purpose.

And I want that for you too. I want to help you climb the many mountains in your life.

An amazing shift and a rebirth happened when I discovered that I was the common denominator in all my troubles. I was the cause of all my pain, suffering, and struggles. You see, I kept repeating old habits, living in the past, and waiting hopelessly for someone to rescue me. When all that failed, I turned to my religious friends who encouraged me to pray to God, read the scriptures, and follow the path of suffering. But not even the vigorous religious practice I picked up could spare me. My religious friends failed to tell me prayers don't change anything and that it was a myth that prayer could and would change everything. I'm not telling you to not pray to God, in fact your life should become a prayer. But I also want you to know prayer alone won't solve your problems. And no one is spared from the trials of their journey because they are praying. God already gave you all the tools you need for your journey. Asking Him for more while doing nothing to help yourself, will not work. Change must come from within you.

Somewhere along the path of my life, I had lost who I was. I was a stranger in a strange place looking for where I fit in. I did not fit into the family in which I was born. I was different from the moment I took my first breath. I had my own way of being, my own will.

Lying in that hospital bed that morning—all alone—I woke up to the reality that I was indeed the common denominator. I realized that all this time I had the tools I needed to make the climb and all I had to do was look within. All I had to do was learn to love myself. All I had to do was accept the fact that I was the problem and not everyone else. At first, the concept was much too simple for me to grasp. It made me sick to my stomach. Before long my mouth was filled with salty water and suddenly I started vomiting green bile. The stuff that came out of my stomach was a perfect metaphor for how disgusting my life was.

For the first time in my life, I remembered who I was. I would have to learn to let go of the past, complete the new chapters. I had gotten comfortable on the journey. I accepted everything people told me about myself. I took on their judgement of me. I accepted the beliefs my tribal family passed down to me. I allowed society and everyone else to think for me. I hated myself, I judged myself, and I put myself at the bottom of the list.

It was this lack of love for myself that allowed me to experiment with drugs, and alcohol. When that failed to give me the satisfaction and joy I was looking for, I turned to men who were just as broken as I, begging them and demanding that they love me. How selfish of me to be asking someone to give me something they did not possess! I was like a strong-arm robber at a convenient store holding the owner at gun point, demanding he give me the million dollars he does not possess.

In that very moment, I came to the realization that my life was not like a deck of cards and life had not dealt me a bad hand. I concluded that God couldn't save me and the only way He could help me was for me to love myself. The day that you are awakened to the simple fact that you are the cause of your own suffering is going to be the worst day of your life. I want to be honest with you about that. It is tough to face up to that fact; however, when you uncover that you are also the solution, it will become the best day of your life. When I discovered I was the solution I was shocked and scared. How could I have caused myself so much pain? I knew I had to change the way I was living my life. But how? I did not know anyone who was living a life of freedom, joy, and abundance.

Let me share with you the process I went through that helped me climb the many mountains in my life. It's a three-step process:

Step One: Stop! Hunker down and accept responsibility for all of it. You are the cause of all the mountains being built up in your life. You are the cause of your lack of abundance. You are responsible for the bankruptcy and the divorce. You are the cause of all the unhealthy relationships in your life. Yes, YOU are the common denominator in all those parts of your life. I know you're probably shocked to hear this but it's nobody's fault that you forgot who you are or where it is you came from. It's not your ex-husband's problem if you are incapable of looking in your own mirror. Many times in your life you have failed to accept your own short comings. You kept looking to your parents, friends, family, co-workers for love, acceptance and approval. You failed to accept that your life has meaning and purpose and you never bothered to look within for the hero that is there waiting to help you make the climb. Instead, you listened to the enemy in your head. You know…the little critical voice that tells you that you focus way too much on your business, or that it was your fault that the marriage ended. You made a choice to listen to the critic's voice instead of listening to the voice that tells you that you have the power to transform your life. The problem is, you are too busy to stop and listen. You are too busy to look and see what's inside the tool belt you've been wearing around your waist since the day your journey began. You are so busy posting the perfect moment on social media and looking at what a so-called perfect life looks like that you have no time to sit and think. In *The Science Of*

Getting Rich, Wallace D. Wattles says, "The hardest work that man is called upon to do is to think." You have yet to stop and think about the life you want to create. You accepted the life that everyone else created for you. You failed to search for the real you.

Now what you have to do is stop running away from your own power. Stop drinking, smoking, cheating on your spouse, and using prescription drugs as a way to numb the pain. These activities will only treat the symptoms but you will never be cured. You must treat the cause of your depression, pain, and anxiety. One thing I learned while going through this step is that a victim can never make the climb to the other side. They are too weak. The moment the climb gets a little tough they are ready to go back down, just like a dog returning eat the very thing he vomited. Disgusting, right? But that's what you and I do. It's human nature.

If you are in a victim state of mind right now I want to remind you that Elizabeth Smart survived a brutal kidnapping and she was able to get her life back on track. Do you know what that was like for her? I have an idea because I also survived a brutal kidnapping at the age of eleven. Sure, I have some post-traumatic stress from the traumas of the past. But I don't allow it to control my life. I don't allow those events to define me. It's not what happened to you but it's what you do with what happened to you. And let's be honest: it's likely you faced nothing nearly as dramatic as a kidnapping. At least, I hope not

But you have had bad things that happened to you; what are you doing with the traumatic events in your life? Are you using Post Traumatic Stress Syndrome as an excuse, so others can feel sorry for you? Or are you using those events as the groundwork to become the masterpiece that you were meant to be?

You must stop blaming your parents. You are not the only person in the world with an alcoholic mother or father. You are not the only person in the world who's been physically or sexually abused. Tyler Perry was sexually abused, but now he's a mogul in the entertainment industry. Oprah Winfrey as well. Thomas Edison was told he would never be anything and he went on to make the great discoveries that you and I are still benefiting from today. It can be done but only if you dare to try. Stop blaming others and look within for strength and solutions.

Step Two: Move! No, you don't need to call a realtor. Or learn to dance. I mean move by getting outside of your comfort zone. We are all creatures of comfort. You love the same old things, like that ratty pair of jeans you pull on every Saturday. You don't want anything to change but the reality is, everything changes sooner or later, whether you are aware of it or not. Nothing stays the same forever. Your favorite neighbor moves away, your child learns new things, the company you work for closes down. Change is inevitable so you have to become fluid and go with the currents of life instead of always fighting against it.

Human beings change every fifteen months. The person you are today is not who you were two years ago. You have to step out of your comfort zone and do the things that are uncomfortable. Meet your new neighbor. Be proud that your child is growing up. Find a new (better) job. When you are following your intuition, and listening to the little friend inside of your head instead of the nasty little critic, you will get inspirations that are not comfortable. But the only way you will succeed is to follow them. You have to learn how to be comfortable with being uncomfortable. Does that make sense? Welcome and enjoy that little flutter in your belly that means excitement is afoot. It's scary but it's exhilarating. Embrace the exhilaration, and ignore the fear factor!

There are several small steps you can take when it comes to getting out of your comfort zone. You can find a mentor, someone who has overcome their own struggles. I'm not talking about someone who paints a picture that everything in their life is perfect. No one has the perfect life; that's a myth you shouldn't chase after. But we all have the ability to create the life we want and desire. It's easier to get out of your comfort zone if you know someone who has paved the way. Many of my cousins who left the tribal family after I left told me I had somehow paved the way for them to follow. If you want to get healthy and you've never run a marathon, hire a fitness coach to help you train. If you are wanting to create a life of freedom, joy, and abundance, work with someone who has done just that. If you want to find a meaningful relationship, work with a relationship coach.

It bears repeating: Get out of your comfort zone and do the things that are uncomfortable. Having been mentored by so many great coaches, I know the freedom, joy, and abundance I'm experiencing in my life today is because they made me do things that were very uncomfortable. Their mentoring made me grow as a person. As a child, whenever I complained about how uncomfortable I was, my grandmother gave me a gentle reminder. She would sarcastically say to me, "If it doesn't kill you, it will make you stronger." This was her way of telling me to get over myself. Most of what we fear comes nowhere near killing us. But even the tragedy and sadness of losing a loved one, which we all fear, can make us stronger by causing us to stand on our own, without them.

Your comfort zone is your own prison. You see, I stayed in my own prison all those years. I stayed with my tribal family because I did not want to step outside of what was 'comfortable' and well-known for me. It's why women stay with abusive men, and children defend abusive parents. We fear the unknown. But if you are not happy with where you are, and you want to move somewhere else, for goodness sake just do it. Don't take the safest and most known path. Choose challenge over comfort and set goals that force you to get out of your comfort zone. To succeed in life, you have to learn how to be comfortable with being uncomfortable.

Step Three: Commit! Commit to doing things differently. Commitment is what will help you achieve whatever goals you set. Notice I said goals, and not resolutions. If you are committed, you will get the results you desire. Maybe it won't be quick, and for sure it won't be the easiest thing you've ever done, but you will succeed if you commit to success.

The only reason you cannot find the person who is right for you is because you are not committed. You have to commit to loving yourself first and putting yourself and your wellbeing above the needs of others. That doesn't mean you don't help the people you love and care about. It simply means you don't sacrifice your own dreams, goals, and desires to please others. I know firsthand what that's like. I married my ex-husband to please my mother. I married him to make my mother happy because I so badly wanted to fit in to a culture and tribe that did not support the person I am today. That was then; this is now. I would never do such a crazy thing again. I am committed to my own freedom, joy, and abundance. You should be committed too.

In the hospital bed that morning the hard truth hit me that everything my ex-husband did to me, I deserved. I was forced to look at my own darkness. I had spent the past three months complaining about how selfish this man was, but yet I was just as selfish. I married him for all the wrong reasons. We always think we are better than the other person. The truth is, we are not. As much as we like to blame the other person, it is our own doing. Remember: You are the common denominator in all your life's little dramas. You are the star of the show.

The more I thought about my life, the worse things got for me. Just when things seemed to be under control with my body, I resumed the vomiting, but now nothing was coming up. If you've ever had them, 'dry heaves' are the worst! The doctor feared I was now suffering from dehydration and electrolyte imbalances. They needed to fix these imbalances right away or I would for sure have the heart attack I feared. After a couple of liters of fluid and the replacement of my potassium and magnesium, I once again cheated death.

But this time I was committed to fixing the imbalances in my life as well. I made a commitment right then and there that the next time death knocked on my door, I would be ready for the journey. And once they handed me the discharge papers, I was committed to living my life on my own terms. I became committed to living according to my higher self. The self that knows and understands that the challenges we face are all part of the journey. You have to develop the muscles necessary to stay in the game. You must have grit and determination. For right now, though, just commit to not quitting until you get the result you desire.

Commitment is the step that changes everything. You can dream of having a wonderful partner. You can visualize it but if you are not committed to creating it, it's never going to happen. Every day for the rest of your life you need to commit to loving yourself and being kind to yourself. This means doing something for you. This means getting the right amount of sleep. This means feeding your body the right food. This means saying no to the people who are sucking the life out of you.

Vince Lombardi said this: "Most people fail, not because of lack of desire, but because of lack of commitment." The next time failure shows up at your doorstep, remember you failed because you were never really committed. That's a hard mirror to look into.

I warned you it would hard, didn't I? But you're worth it!

Chapter 2
Give Yourself a Gift!

As we know, you are worth the best that life has to offer, so don't hesitate to give yourself a wonderful gift: *Forgiveness.* It may not come wrapped in a blue Tiffany box, but it may just be the most valuable gift you've ever received. And as a bonus, it will cost you nothing other than a large dose of humility, spiced up with a healthy sprinkling of honesty. No need to wait for your birthday or Christmas – do it today.

If you've ever gotten some inspiration to improve yourself, or done any form of self-development work, it won't be long before someone tells you about forgiveness. Forgiveness is the one tool in your tool belt that you can use to set yourself free from all forms of lack and suffering. If you want to be free, you have to forgive the people who have caused you a great deal of pain. The only way to let go of the past is to forgive those who have not been kind to you. Jesus, the great teacher, instructed His followers to forgive one another and as He took His last breath he prayed, "Father, forgive them for they know not what they do." That is the gift He gave to each of us: the ability to forgive.

For more than a decade, I stayed anchored to my pain and hurt, holding it close like a talisman, a bulletproof shield that would not allow anyone or anything to pierce through it. I pridefully carried injuries from the past with me just as I would have some precious memorabilia given to me by a loved one. How I longed to not lose the memories of how I escaped a near rape by my own uncle, or the brutal beatings I suffered at the hands of my brother. How I savored the pain, remembering the three darkest days of my life spent in the woods with the madman who'd kidnapped me. How angry I was at my mother for not protecting me from the predators in my life. It was her job, I believed, and she had failed miserably. So long as I kept blaming her, I could ignore my own part in the drama.

Holding onto that anger gave me a sort of self-satisfaction. It made me feel as if I was better than them. It allowed me to not see my own darkness, and it fueled my desire to stay bitter. Somehow, I had made the choice to be an angry person. I had the right to be angry, after all the things that had been done to me. Poor me. So, I dragged those hurts like a ball and chain, even when they caused me even more injury. They were *mine;* I owned them. No one could deprive me of my pathetic baggage. Is that you? Are you hanging onto past hurts with self-righteous outrage? It's time to find a locksmith and cut the chain loose!

I want to remind you that everything you've experienced in this lifetime you singed up for. I want to caution you against the belief that we don't choose our parents. It's a complete lie that we are all innocent bystanders when it comes to our own incarnation. We are not innocent bystanders. You chose your incarnation just like I chose mine. Each and everyone of us choose our incarnation based on the lessons our soul needs in this lifetime. I absolutely know this to be true – it has been revealed to me many times with clarity. But don't just take my word for it.

If you're interested in this concept, you can (and should) read Neale Donald Walsch's book *The Little Soul in the Sun.* After reading his work, I know I chose my mother. Despite my troubled relationship with her, I still credit her for the person I am today. If you had the opportunity to meet my mother and get to know me personally, you would come to your own conclusion: I'm the mirror image of my mother. Though my mother has put me through hell, in order to advance in my journey, I had to forgive her and all the other people who have caused me pain. You cannot move forward if you are bound and chained by past hurts. Let them go.

Forgiveness is not a gift you give to the people who have hurt you. It's a gift you give to yourself. As long as you remain in victim mode, giving yourself permission to be injured, you cannot begin the process of forgiveness. Forgiveness is a three-step process and I'm going to walk you through this process and give you some practical things you can do to start the journey of forgiveness.

Step One: Acceptance Accept the anger, the pain, and the resentment. It is part of you. Accept it. Don't try to numb it with drinking, shopping, overeating, or any other negative behavior that leads to self-destruction. You must acknowledge that you are angry and that you accept the anger. And it's okay to be angry and you can be angry for a time; just remember you can't stay there for the next decade of your life. It may help to set a time limit.

I know it goes against social norms to be angry; according to today's societal norms, you're supposed to be happy all the time, even when your world is falling apart. You can easily see this unrealistic expectation on FaceBook, where we past happy faces and smiling stickers on every post. Everyone is eager to share the perfect moment, the perfect child, or the perfect outing. When you dare post the struggles you are really facing, you don't find many motivational words coming forth that can help you deal with the trials and tribulations you face. The truth is, nobody has many encouraging words for you except perhaps 'don't give up'. What exactly does that mean? It's like telling a baby to stop crying but a baby won't stop crying unless his or her needs are met. Your friends on FaceBook don't give a damn about your painful issues. They have their own crosses to bear. Most of them won't share it on FaceBook because they are too busy looking for the next perfect moment in their lives to hide their pain. And so the phony pretense is perpetuated, post after post, never revealing honesty. Do not look to social media for honesty or truth. You will most often be disappointed. Social media, however, is great for meeting people and learning about events.

Unrealistic expectations, fostered by fake posts on social media, causes you to not be in touch with your anger, sadness, and disappointment. Don't get me wrong, I'm all for joy, peace, love, happiness, and abundance. But let's be realistic: you are not going to experience these emotions every single day of your life. I don't care how much money you have, some days you're going to feel sad or down about certain aspects of your life. It's unrealistic to think that you can be happy every single day. No one is ever happy and blissful year 'round.

The guru that paints his or herself as having the perfect life is not being truthful. Everyone's got challenges and situations they have to overcome. Even the wealthiest superstar or sports giant has problems. You might be struggling with depression, while another person is being dragged to court in a custody battle. Another might be caring for their ailing mother who is suffering from cancer or dementia. Yet another might have lost his wife during the child-bearing process. It's called life. It isn't perfect for anyone.

Circumstances in your life can agitate you, like a washing machine on the scrub cycle. Do you have a right to be pissed off, hurt, and angry? Of course you do! When someone hurts you, you have every right to be pissed off and angry because betrayal doesn't feel good. So be angry and pissed off, just remember at some point in time you simply must move past the anger. Consider it a temporary obstacle in your path that you will acknowledge, then move past.

Today I'm going to tell you that anger is your friend. Anger is not your enemy. You have the right to be sad about certain aspects of your life. Sadness is also your friend and not your enemy. Disappointment and failure are your friends as well. Every single emotion that you experience is your friend. Accept them. Your sadness has special messages for you. On the days that you are sad, take a minute to talk to the sadness. Ask your friend, "Sadness, what message do you have for me today?" Ask your friend, "Anger, what message do you have for me today?" Spend time with these emotions and you will get a better understanding of the areas of your life that are out of balance.

I have learned so much from my anger! I was so angry I was like a walking time bomb waiting to go off. The anger affected every area of my life and one day I chose to ignore everyone's advice to 'just be happy'. The truth is, I didn't know how to be happy. I could never be happy until I dealt with my anger. I could see happy down the path, but I couldn't get past the obstacle of anger to get to it.

One day I sat down and I asked my anger a question: "How do we become friends?"

What I discovered when I started sitting with my anger really surprised me. Underneath the anger was a young woman drowning in apathy. I discovered my ability to be content with who I am and where I am in every stage of my journey. I learned all that was getting to know and understand my anger. It was justified but didn't deserve to rule my life.

My husband often tells me it doesn't take much to make me happy. And he is right. My happiness is a state of being for me. Underneath the anger lies a cheerful person, a grateful person, a woman eager to change the course of her life and rewrite her story with a happy ending. My (friend) anger has helped me accept myself and others. Anger has taught me to make peace with myself and the world around me. It was my anger that helped me get to a place where I can be my authentic self. What will you discover about yourself when you accept your sadness, anger, pain, and resentment? I challenge you to accept these emotions and spend time with them; I promise that once you do, the universe will transform your life.

Step Two: Forgiveness Forgive yourself and those who have wronged you. The first person in line for forgiveness is YOU. How many times have you said, "How could I have been so stupid? How come I did not see this?" The questions asked as if you're supposed to be able to foresee everything coming down the pipeline. I hope you know the universe will only show you the first twenty-steps and nothing else will ever be revealed to you until you take the first twenty-steps. I don't know about you, but in my opinion that's not showing at all. The point is, we make mistakes and that's a simple fact you have to accept. You are not perfect and you will never be perfect. You and I are humans and we screw things up. As a matter of fact, it's our job to screw things up. But it's also our job to learn the lessons, forgive ourselves, and move on.

The relationship you have with yourself is the most important relationship you will ever have. If you want to create a meaningful relationship with someone else, you better start creating that relationship with yourself first. You must be kind to yourself. It's your job to forgive yourself.

Let go of what you did or didn't do. Let go of what you should have done. Let go of the past. For many years after the kidnapping, I blamed myself for letting a madman talk me into getting in his car. It wasn't my fault but I blamed myself for it anyway. I blamed myself for escaping a near rape by my own uncle. I kept blaming myself for going over to his house in the middle of the day when no one was home. Perhaps if I had not gone over there alone that would never have happened. Remember the little critic's voice in our head? It really isn't our friend, is it; however, when I started listening to the little *friendly* voice in my head, she was quick to remind me that my uncle was full of demons and if it wasn't me he raped, it was going to be someone else. Stop blaming yourself, because until you do that, you won't have the courage to climb out of the rubble. It takes a strong person to forgive and let go of the past. But it takes a wise and courageous person to practice forgiveness for themselves. Every single day of your life you get an opportunity to choose who you want to be. The question is: Who do you really want to be? Do you want to be weak or do you want to be strong? You may think you are being strong by holding on to the garbage of the past. Mahatma Gandhi said, "The weak can never forgive. Forgiveness is the attribute of the strong." Ouch, that really hurts!

I used to think I was strong by holding on to all the baggage of the past but really, I was placing myself in an emotional prison. When you made the decision to not forgive yourself, along with those who harmed you, in that very moment you placed yourself in an emotional prison. When was the last time you saw an inmate enjoying a life of freedom, joy, and abundance? They are in a physical prison but many of us are captured in an emotional prison. This process explains why only ten percent of the population experiences true happiness. There are definitely gains to holding on to the pain of the past. If there was no benefit to it, we would not hold on. Everything we do is because we get something out of it. But what exactly do you gain from your inability to forgive yourself and others? By not practicing forgiveness, you get to sit with the anger, pain, and resentment for the rest of your life. A child who wets the bed is much more comfortable being very still in the warm wetness, than moving to a spot that is dry but cold. This concept explains why you can meet someone who experienced tragedy and years later they are still talking about the hell they went through as if it happened yesterday. And when you ask them how long it has been they say, "Oh gosh, it's been fifteen years." Have you ever met one of those people? Next time you meet one of them please hand them a copy of this book!

You also have a hard time practicing forgiveness because you get to feel good about yourself; virtuous. It makes you feel like you're better than the people who have hurt you. But you're not. That's just a lie you tell yourself to avoid moving. You're just another human being just like him or her. Your ego loves the feeling of being better than someone else. The ego loves it when you stay stuck in the past. The future you want to create is not created in the past, it's created in the present moment. And since the ego doesn't like change, it couldn't care less about the future you want to create. The ego is more than happy to keep you exactly where you are. By making the choice to not forgive, you've placed yourself an in emotional prison. And guess what? Your ego rejoices, because it knows there will never be any change. Staying safely locked in prison is easier than moving forward into the unknown. But joy is not in that prison cell; you have to get out of jail to find it!

What are you losing by holding on to the hurts of the past? You lose your sense of peace. A lack of peace equals confusion and a lack of clarity. When you are not able to forgive, you are stuck in the past and so you lose the ability to set a course of action for the future. You wonder why you are in the same spot you where in five or even ten tears ago. You wonder why it's so difficult for you to find someone to share your life with. It's all because you choose to hold on to the past. You might be divorced from your husband but if you have not forgiven him, you are still emotionally tied to him. You wonder why you are having such a hard time finding your Mr. Right. How about closing the previous chapter first? Get rid of Mr. Wrong to make room for the right partner.

Step Three: Let go! Release it. Set it free. You have got to let it go. It's the only way for you to find peace. So many of us fall into the trap of believing that if we forgive someone, it means we must suddenly embrace them or trust them. No! Forgiveness and trust are two separate subjects. Forgiveness cannot be earned. It can only be given; however, trust can't be given, it can only be earned.

When someone you trust betrays you, and you give them your forgiveness, can you trust them ever again? That's a personal choice for you to make. I can never again trust my uncle, though I have forgiven him. He is not someone I want at my dinner table. I have forgiven my brother for the brutal beatings; however, I have made a personal decision to never again break bread with either of these men. Forgiveness doesn't mean you need to invite them back into your life and allow them to hurt you over and over again. I know people who have done that and in my professional opinion, I believe only those who don't love themselves allow others to abuse them. Forgiveness goes from you to them; it doesn't make the roundtrip ticket. Whether you ever let them into your inner circle again is your decision. Make it carefully. Just because you forgive someone, which is necessary for your forward progress, does not mean they get a second chance. Second chances must be earned.

This third step in the process is not at all hard and once you make the decision to move forward, and you are committed, it becomes effortless. In every single situation, I challenge you to practice forgiveness for yourself and for the other person. Forgiveness is a gift you give yourself. It's not a gift you're giving to your partner, mother, friend, etc. According to Maya Angelo, it's the biggest gift you give yourself. Forgiveness is what will allow you to access your higher self so you can create the relationships you want. Whatever it is you want to create, you have to set yourself free of the emotional prison that you're in so that you can gain clarity and peace. Remember: Forgiveness doesn't change the past but it will free you from the burden of regrets and resentment. It's the ultimate Get Out of Jail Free card.

You want a life of freedom, joy, and abundance, right? Stop bitching and complaining and practice forgiveness. It's the gift you can give yourself again and again; there's no expiration date!

Chapter 3
Put Your Ego Aside.

Or, as my son would say, "Leggo my ego!"

To create a life of freedom, joy, and abundance—the life you dream of—you must learn how to put your ego aside. "What's that?" you ask? Well, I can assure you it's not a breakfast food! It also doesn't mean "conceit" as many people assume. Everyone has an ego but that doesn't mean they think highly of themselves. I can actually be the opposite.

So let's talk about the ego for a moment. The ego is an identity of your own construction. It's a made-up sense of self; an identity which is not the true essence of who you are but rather an invented identity. In other words, it is a false identity you've given yourself. The ego is the mental construction of yourself. It's the artificial 'Self.' And being artificial and self-made, it can be remade.

When you have thoughts about yourself that you agree with, you construct a self image that reflects your positive thoughts. "I look great today." And so, you go about your day feeling beautiful and you act with confidence.

Or perhaps you think, "I don't deserve this treatment. I'm better than you." In that case, you react to negative treatment with another negative thought. Basically, you manifest what you think. All the chatter in your head is really your ego talking. I call it the little critic.

Remember my 'wee hours of the morning' visit to the ER with a panic attack? I'll never forget it. After getting my discharge papers from the hospital, I was committed to creating a life of freedom, joy, and abundance. Though I was optimistic about the possibility of creating a new life for myself, my ego was full of questions for me.

My conversations with myself went something like this: "Oh, yeah? How are you going to create a life of freedom, joy, and abundance when you are bankrupt?" My inner little critic was skeptical, negative, and constantly challenged my intentions. My ego (little critic) was trying to protect me *by keeping me static, in the same place, and not making any big changes in my life.*

Despite my ego, I really wanted to create that life of freedom, joy, and abundance. I had no idea how I was going to do that, but luckily for me I chose to listen to the other little voice in my head—I call that the good angel—that constantly reminded me that I could do more, be more, and have more. Before you can uncover who you *really* are, you have to first understand your ego. Let me briefly introduce you to the ego.

The ego likes the status quo and wants nothing to do with change. The last thing your ego wants is for you to create the relationships you desire. Your ego does not want you to create a life of freedom, joy, and abundance. The ego will remind you constantly that freedom and abundance is for those who are lucky. According to your ego, you don't have to work for it, you just need to be lucky. And you're not lucky, it tells you. Your ego doesn't care about your dreams or your desires. The ego has one objective: To keep you stuck in the warm gooey mud. Have you ever in your life felt stuck? Or as if your situation was hopeless? That's what happens to women who are abused but stay with their abuser. Their ego tells them it's an even scarier world out there without Johnny, so just hang in there. He will change. So if you've ever felt this way, it's because your ego has blinded you to the truth of what's possible for you.

The ego has many secret weapons. He is like a ninja. He comes at you quick and fast. A single blow to the head and you have no time to process what just happened. One of the ego's greatest weapons is fear. He uses fear to paralyze you, like a cripple who can't manage to get out of bed in the morning, you can't seem to escape the many crises in your life. The mountains in your life are so scary that instead of attempting the climb, you choose to walk away. You choose to ignore them as if they will magically disappear. You label yourself as unlucky. You tell yourself all kinds of false stories to keep yourself in that warm mud. You feel you know the mud very well, up close and personal, but the world outside the mud might be even worse. So you stay stuck.

You are not unlucky at all; your ego is working relentlessly to keep you stuck. If you are not careful, you will remain there for the rest of your miserable life. The ego likes it when you are miserable because when you are miserable you will bitch and complain and become the victim of the circumstances you have created for yourself. "Poor me, poor me." You tell your friends about your misery and they share it with other friends and relatives and before you know it, your friends and neighbors are saying, "That poor kid can't seem to catch a break." Their sympathy reinforces your ego's presumption that your situation is not your fault; you are just unlucky in business, unlucky in love, and/or unlucky in life.

The ego will use fear to turn your life upside down and keep you exactly where you are. Fear will grab you like a thief in the night and unless you fight back you will become as helpless as a newborn baby. Fear will cause you to turn to religion for refuge and looking to God to help you with very little effort expended on your part. What happens when you do this? You will become like my tribal family, believing that there's a superior force fighting against you. Every single step you take to get out of the mud, he is there to make sure you take three steps backward. You become a crap magnet, attracting all the things you feared the most. Your only hope will be the "someday" sermon that Christ is coming back to take you to the Promised Land and there you will live happily ever after. No need to do anything for yourself; God will come and pull you out of your mud pit.

Even if that is true, why can't you be happy right now? Why can't you have the life you want and desire in *this* lifetime? Why would God create this beautiful planet and add people who are created in His image, simply to have them suffer? What kind of God does that? I don't believe He does. I believe He wants you out of that mud, living a life of freedom, joy, and abundance.

Even as a child, I refused to accept that theory sold to me by my tribal family. Are you ready to hear the truth? There is no adversary working against you. There is no enemy and no you don't have to put on the armor of God like the Bible instructs. What you *must* do instead is to stop looking inside the envelope that says: "The poverty you will have" and start looking inside the envelope that says: "The riches you will possess." I wish I could take credit for this, but the brilliant Napoleon Hill talked about this very concept in his book *Think Rich and Grow Rich*. Hill challenges his readers to simply change their thinking. I challenge you to do the same. When you start thinking the right way, you will recognize that there never was an enemy and that the only enemy is you, yourself, and your ego. Shocking, isn't it?

Indeed, the enemy is you. It's your ego. It's the way you think. The way you run your affairs. The enemy is your habits. The enemy is the hurt, the pain, the jealousy, and resentment you hold in your heart. The enemy is the negative thoughts you choose to entertain twenty-four hours a day, seven days a week, and three hundred sixty-five days a year. The enemy is your inability to forgive yourself and those who have harmed you. The enemy is the position you have taken in life. It's the way you view and think about your life. The enemy is your refusal to change, to accept change, and go with the flowing currents of life. This, my dear friend, is the only enemy and it's the only enemy there will ever be. Lucifer was cast into the fires of hell many centuries ago. Stop believing there's a devil or an outside force working against you. Remember the common denominator? You are the cause of all of it. Swallow your pride and if you don't like the life you have created, make a commitment to change it.

I often hear my religious friends and family make statements such as, "The enemy is strong." What enemy are you talking about? Of course, the enemy is strong. Do you not know how powerful you are? Do you not know that you create every single experience you have in this lifetime? When you made an unconscious choice not to think for yourself, then you made a choice to allow others to think for you. When you are too lazy to come up with your own belief system, you allow religion, friends, and family to do the thinking for you. The results you are getting when you listen to them, are the same results they are getting. Do you want a replica of their lives, or do you want your own life of freedom, joy, and abundance? If you want a different result you are going to have to start thinking for yourself.

Here's what Wallace D. Wattles had to say on the matter of thinking: *"Man is a thinking center, and can originate thought. All forms that man fashions with his hands must first exist in his thoughts; he cannot shape a thing until he has thought that thing through."*

Every single thing on Earth that has ever been created BEGAN WITH A THOUGHT. That's how powerful our thoughts are!

Your life will not change until you sit down and think about the life you want to create for yourself. You will not have the partnership you want until you formulate a picture in your mind of what that looks like to you. Because you fail to use your power to think the correct thoughts, instead of creating a life of freedom, joy, and abundance for yourself, you've created many mountains of the very things you don't want. You created your mud pit. Now you must create a vision of a beautiful life outside that mud pit, and then move toward it.

Your words carry weight. Let me give you an example of the power of words. When I was eleven years old, I made up a story about what my life was going to be like when I got older. I kept telling my family how someday I was going to make eighty thousand dollars. During that time, I was obsessed with *Jurassic Park*. I must have read the book a hundred times. I later learned that the movie had been filmed in Hawaii. I would tell everyone how I was going to go to Hawaii to see The Wall of Tears. I told this grand story about moving to California and living within walking distance of the Golden Gate Bridge. I became the laughing stock of the neighborhood called Little Haiti in Miami. My mother had four children and she made fifteen thousand dollars a year. The room I remember most from our small house was called our 'living room' but it was actually more of a dying room. It was a tiny charmless hollow square space, lit only by one puke green junk-store lamp, so it was always dark, even on the sunniest Miami day. I think my mom bought that hideous ceramic lamp at the Goodwill Store; it was cracked and the cord was dangerously frayed. A filthy ruined brown carpet assured the darkness, and a three-legged coffee table anchored the space. No one ever dared to set a cup of coffee on it for fear it would collapse. My childhood home was not very inspirational or encouraging. How in the world was I going to accomplish my dreams?

Most days we were lucky if we even got a meal. But whenever my mom and siblings had friends over, they would call me into the 'living room' and make me tell my story. I was excited to tell the story. I was passionate about the story and in my child's mind it was all possible, even in that dark dreary space I used for a stage. And always after I told the story everyone would laugh. I mean, you know the kind of laugh, when people are falling over and tears are coming from their eyes, and they have a bellyache from laughing so hard. It was that kind of laughter. I performed for them like a comedy actress but without the pay. I still remember the day it dawned on me that they were laughing at me because they didn't believe it was possible. I cried myself to sleep that night. I stopped telling the story but I continued to read the book.

They laughed because they didn't believe it was possible for me because it was not possible for them. How many times have you allowed other people to tell you what's possible for you? How many times have you allowed other people to kill your dreams? Fast forward nineteen years and there I was, living six miles away from the Golden Gate Bridge. For five years, I jogged across that bridge at least three times a week for fitness sake. And oh, let's not forget The Wall of Tears. I flew over it in a helicopter on a Hawaiian vacation with my husband. The eighty-thousand-dollar yearly salary? I doubled that before I turned thirty.

What are you passionate about? What do you think about before turning off your light at night?

Your passion is the paint brush painting the life that you desire. The things you think about are the things you are creating. What is it that you really desire? What does your heart long for? I dare you to explore new possibilities for yourself while ignoring the ego, who's telling you how crazy you are. And let's not forget your friends and family, who will certainly validate the negative thoughts the ego is telling you. Misery, after all, does love company.

The ego will gently tap you on the shoulder in the middle of the night to remind you that you don't have the house that you want, but that's okay. You're not lucky. The ego will not fail to remind you how you got passed up for the promotion. But that's okay; you weren't ready for that career move. The ego will tell you how you don't have the money or the resources you need to start your own business. The ego will tell you that you are too old to find a life partner. The ego will remind you that love is a fairytale story and your life is that of a Shakespearean tragedy.

Your ego is fearless and it will not be afraid to tell you to settle for less. Your ego will make you settle for a piece of a man. Your ego will tell you to accept his randomized efforts at affection because waiting for a whole man is like waiting for mana to fall out of the sky. If you listen to your ego, there is no end to the rabbit holes where the ego will take you. I have personally learned to laugh at the lies my ego tells me about my life. I have chosen to ignore the ego with all its negative folly. When you start laughing at the lies, only then will you be able to create a life of freedom, joy, and abundance. It all begins in your mind, recognizing the ego's voice when it speaks crap to you, and instead of taking it seriously, you laugh and move forward with your better ideas.

Freedom is there for everyone who wants to experience it. Abundance is waiting for everyone to experience; the choice is yours. It took laying in a hospital bed for me to discover that there is no enemy. There never was, and there never will be. The 'enemy' was my very own ego. The artificial self that I created blinded me from the truth of who I was and what I could achieve. It's one thing when you discover that you are the cause of your own pain and suffering, but it's another thing when you discover there is no devil. There is no good or bad. There simply is. It's one energy manifesting itself in many different forms. The things you experience in your life are based on the form of energy you have tapped into. Honestly, it's that simple.

In order to transform my life, I had to stop tapping into the lesser form of this energy. I had to start tapping into the beauty of this energy. It's an energy that is within us of all, not just the 'lucky'. I had to become aware of its compassion for me and the rest of the human race. I had to surrender my ego and return to my state of the eager child who once thought she could conquer the world. And pretty soon, I learned that there was no limit to my abilities and capabilities.

What do you believe?

Do you believe that something or someone is keeping you from creating the life you desire? If so, I want you to take a hard look in the mirror at your ego. I want you to consider putting your ego aside, even if it's just until you can create what you desire. I want you to learn the power that exists within you. This substance that lives in you, this amazing creation, is called *you*. You can overcome every single hardship. You can rise out of the ashes over and over again, just like the mythical Phoenix.

Are you up for a blind date?

I'm sure you are asking, "How do I get in touch with this substance? What exactly happens when you decide to put your ego aside?"

Let me introduce you to the humble and wise helper you will meet. I promise it will be the best blind date you ever had! Meet your dream boat: Your subconscious mind. Unlike your ego, this mind is very humble. Your subconscious mind knows the truth of who you are and where it is you came from. This mind allows you to choose your own path. It doesn't compete with anything or anyone. This mind will never force you to look down rabbit holes for him. He wants the best for you and won't tell you lies like "stay in the nice warm mud." But if you look within, he will be right there to guide you on your path. This mind sits quietly and waits for you to ask for help. This mind knows he is all powerful and all knowing. Unlike your ego, this mind does not need to prove its power. Instead, he *owns* his power. It's the little voice that whispers to you when there's danger. It's sometimes called your "gut instincts" or "women's intuition".

This is the mind that knows all there is to know. He knows he is a master and doesn't need anything tangible to prove it. This mind never competes for anything because it has everything. This mind requires nothing from you or me but is willing to help us create anything we fathom in our mind. This is the mind that consistently whispered to me, "Naomi, you're better than this. Naomi, do more, be more." And during the dark nights in my soul this mind gently whispers, "All is well." This is the voice you must listen to.

This mind has no identity. It doesn't identify itself based on material success. This mind won't allow you to compare yourself with others. Instead, it sets you on your own course and allows you to see yourself as the light and loving being that you truly are. This mind is not afraid to be alone. In the moment of your loneliness, this mind weaves the fabric for the masterpiece he is going to turn you into. This mind is capable of turning your sorrows into joy, your losses into great gains, and your failures into successes. It's the only mind that will never judge you. It's the mind that will help you love every aspect of who you are. The good, the bad, and the ugly.

When the blind date turns into a love affair.

How exactly do you access this beautiful mind? You have to be willing to put your ego aside. When you are working with this mind, your past is irrelevant. You become the author of your own story. To get to know this mind, you just have to create space in your consciousness for it. The more you become aware of the existence of this great mind, the quicker you will be able to access it. Everything starts with awareness. If you don't believe this mind is real, I invite you to do some research. Many great scholars talk about this mind. In *The Master Key*

System written by Charles Haanel over a hundred years ago, he teaches us exactly how to get in touch with this mind. In fact, it was his body of work that helped me unlock my own powers.

When it comes to the belief that there's some external force that is messing things up for us, here's what Charles Haanel said: *"Our future is entirely within our own control. It is not at the mercy of any capricious or uncertain external power."*

To access the subconscious mind, you must learn to quiet your own mind (ego). In fact, if you ever decide to dive deeply into Haanel's work the first thing he teaches you is to learn to sit still and quiet the mind. Such a hard thing to do in today's society with all the social media we are bombarded with! But it's critical to make time to sit in the silence. The silence is the only place you will ever meet this mind. You see, this mind is the master of peace, love, and harmony. It can never thrive in chaos. Yet your life is like a crazy reality show without the paycheck or TMZ following you around with a camera! Or like a Shakespearean comedy without the laughter. How do you suppose you will ever find the answers to the questions you are asking? How do you suppose you will ever climb the mountains in your life or get out of the mud pit if you are not willing to sit and listen? You have to want to know who you are in order to discover who you are. You have to be thirsty for knowledge in order for you to become wise. I was thirsty for it because I'm not patient enough to wait for the second coming of Christ to experience a life of freedom, joy, and abundance. *I want it now in this lifetime.* It's my birthright. Don't you want that too? I hope you will want it badly enough to carve out some time to get to know yourself.

After my ex-husband took off, I sat for hours in the empty house reflecting on where I had been and where I was headed. To be honest, there was nothing to distract me; no TV, radio, or other pacifier. So I turned inward. It was in that very moment that I met this great mind. It was our first date, so to speak. And I liked him immediately.

This mind embraced me and welcomed me home. My ego fought like a great warrior to keep this reunion from happening. My mind often wanders. The ego, through his weapons of fear, doubt, shame, regret, and confusion, attacked me all at once. It created chaos to thwart my conversation with my beautiful mind. But this mind constantly reminded me of my true essence. That's what happens when you sit still and connect with who you are. This is the great battle of the good versus the evil. The light versus the dark. Someone is going to win but it is *you* who gets to determine the winner. By now, I think you have a clue as to who you want to win that battle, or you would not be reading this book.

Arming yourself for the battle.

Truth is, you have to be *fierce*. You cannot waiver in your decision or your determination. Prepare yourself for this great battle. How? You start by reading books, repeating affirmations, and daily visualizing what you want.

Most people will lose the battle before it begins. They sit for a few days and they get nothing and then give up. "I don't hear anything, I don't feel anything." Some sit for a few months and just when their ego is starting to die, they decide it's not working. It took years of building this false identity for yourself and it's going to take time to build a new sense of self. Be patient with the process. It took me a full year of sitting quietly *every single day* to get in touch with my subconscious mind. I had twenty-five years of false self to undo. You might have thirty years or fifty years of false self to undo, but just know it can be done. I believe you have what it takes to create the life you desire. You have what it takes to create the partnership you desire. All you have to do is turn your focus within.

Start today. "Leggo that Ego!" Don't let the ego tell you "you have no time" or "you will not succeed." Ignore that false voice. Find your Right and True Self.

It's all in your power. In your hands. In your own beautiful mind.

Chapter 4
Non-negotiable Boundaries

It sounds like the worst sort of cliché: You don't know what you don't know. But like most all clichés, it is rooted in truth. The fact that most of life's mysteries are hidden from us is all part of the journey, right? If we knew for sure what was ahead on our pathway, we might just be too scared to take a step forward! Or we would be so excited we would race ahead and miss out on the "now". But lurking out there are answers to questions we don't even know to ask.

Truth is: We are here to fumble along, make mistakes, and *learn* from them. That doesn't mean we can't also learn from the mistakes of those who came before us. Our parents told us that all the time, as we say it to our kids: Learn from my mistakes. I want to give you an opportunity to learn from one of mine.

It was late September; early morning rays of sunlight filtered through the big oval window in my bedroom, reflecting on the old, dark mahogany nightstand. The sun streamed in like an impatient guest, ready to start the day. "Get up!" it was saying. "It's a beautiful day." But I pulled a pillow over my head and ignored the growing sunlight.

For the first time in years, I had slept in. My mind knew it was time to get up but my body was in a state of exhaustion from all the festivities of the previous night. You have probably heard the expression: Every girl deserves to be a princess for the day. Well, the day before, I had indeed been a princess but no one told me the cost to be paid for being a princess for a day.

I rolled over and bumped against a handsome six-foot two light-skinned man whom I believed with all my heart was my Prince Charming. The shining knight in armor I was going to escape off into the sunset with and live happily ever after. I wish someone had told me that my Prince Charming was like all humans: He made mistakes. He was quite flawed. In fact, he was more frog than prince.

After kissing many frogs, I thought I could recognize them. And this man was not a frog; I was going to spend the rest of my life with him. He didn't look like a frog to me then but little did I know, frogs came in all colors, shapes, and sizes. Yes, they can disguise themselves as princes, and frequently do.

But I was so sure of his prince-hood that the day before I made the biggest promise of my life. I had raised my right hand and said my wedding vows. I meant every single word of them too. After all, what could possibly go wrong? I loved him and he was crazy about me and that was all we need to be blissfully happy for the rest of our lives.

That sunny morning my husband woke up and said: "Finally I have everything I ever wanted."

The feeling was mutual. Not only did I have everything I wanted, I had made my family proud. And I was filled with pride that I had made them proud! I'm sure you know that feeling. You see, in my culture, the expectation is that you graduate high school and you find a husband. I had been rebellious and gone to college so I was already on shaky ground with my family. Then I began a career before finding a husband. I was twenty-six years old and according to my family, I was already an old maid. But my wedding day I was redeemed in their eyes; I was not the family leper who had a degree, a career, and no husband to make me whole. I had a husband now who would keep me on the right path. He would keep me at home, pregnant, and obedient. A good girl.

That morning we kissed, hugged, and did all the things newlyweds do. Though he was much older than I was, neither of us had ever been married and we had no clue what it would take to uphold the promises we had made to each other. Somehow, despite our ages, we just figured it would "happen".
We were both happy to say goodbye to Florida. The year before we were married, I had moved to Buford, Georgia. Georgia, in my mind, was going to be my home and my life was going to be that of a Southern woman with a flare of the life Scarlet O'Hara lived. It should have occurred to me that she was a fictional character, not a real woman. But…oh, well…

Before the wedding, I had purchased a small house with a white picket fence. It wasn't a grand Colonial mansion like Tara by a long shot, but it was a pretty little ranch home on two acres of land. I was very proud of the house and spent a great deal of time remodeling it to my own liking. I put in beautiful carpeting that matched the curtains. The furniture was a reflection of the woman I was becoming. I was happy and excited to bring my new husband into my space. I had now officially achieved the American Dream. Husband, check. Home owner, check.

That first night we slept in the house together I felt a sense of tremendous achievement. My soul was happy and satisfied. Though I had spent a great number of years determined not to follow cultural norms I had now acknowledged that it was indeed a wonderful thing to have a mate, someone with whom you can share your life with.

Just three weeks after we settled into our new home, my Prince Charming began to reveal his...less princely side. What started out as a conversation turned into a yelling match between us which resulted in me spending several nights on the couch. The honeymoon was officially over in a flash and I now had to deal with this faulty human non-prince who told me, "You are my wife and you are going to do as I say."

Woah! I was pissed off beyond words, plus insulted and hurt. I had been a rebel from the time I entered my mother's womb. My attitude was, "Oh, I'll show you!" This resulted in our separating within six months of the wedding day. So much for happily ever, right? I was mad, yes, but I was also disillusioned. This was not what I had signed up for. I wanted the carriage, the golden slipper, and the beautiful prince holding me tight every night. I wanted someone who shared my dreams, and wanted me to be successful. Not someone who would crush them, and demand only servitude.

As children, our families and communities tell us what we are supposed to do. For example, you graduate high school then you go to college. When you graduate college, you have to find a job in your field of studies and shortly there after you find a partner and you get married and have two children. A girl and a boy is preferred. What our families and society gives us is a guideline to what should happen, and in the order they think it should all happen; however, I want to call your attention to the details that are left out. To find true freedom, joy, and abundance you need more than guidelines. You need facts and details. I mean the meat and the potato stuff that's going to help you succeed.

The yelling match between my new husband and me would not have taken place if I had had more details. If I had known what I know now I would have set boundaries from the very start. Not only would I have set boundaries, I would have set *nonnegotiable* boundaries.

That's what I want to give you today. Let's get to it!

What are boundaries and why do you need them? According to Google, personal boundaries are: guidelines, rules, or limits that a person creates to identity reasonable, safe, and permissible ways for the other person to behave toward them.

Personal boundaries are like fences you erect around you to protect you from being assaulted (like I was by my new husband). You need to be able to tell others how (and how not) to behave toward you. Not just Prince Charming, but everyone who enters your space. This includes the mother you love dearly, your boss, co-workers, and even the people you serve. Without boundaries, you cannot create a life where you are free to do what you want to do and have a joyful life. Living without boundaries is like the Old West with open range grazing. Too often, coyotes and other predators invade the space and cause havoc. Remember the old saying: Good fences make good neighbors.

Good, strong, sensible personal boundaries make not just good neighbors, but good family relationships and a happy life for you filled with freedom, joy, and abundance.

There are two reasons why boundaries are needed:

#1 to let the people in your life know how you want to be treated;

#2 to promote your own growth and development.

I can hear you now wrestling with the voices in your head. "Naomi, you don't know my husband." Or, "Naomi, you don't know my boss. I'll get fired if I say anything to him/her. I need my job."

And you're right. I don't know your husband or your boss. But what I do know is if you don't stand up for yourself, no one else will. No one. Setting non-negotiable boundaries is the only way for you to create the life you desire. The people in your life need to have a clear understanding of how they should treat you. They need to know what these expectations are and what the cost is for not respecting the boundaries you've put in place. You know the cost of running a red light, right?

Every single person in my life knows the cost of crossing the boundary lines I have put in place. They have the right to cross that line if they so choose, but one thing's for sure, they will no longer be able to dwell or play in my space. And they all know my space is pretty awesome (so is yours) and they don't want to be ejected. That, my friend, is called self-love. When you love yourself, you don't allow anyone to make you feel less than you are. When you love yourself, you don't allow anyone to tell you what's possible for you and what's not possible for you. When you fall in love with yourself, you set up boundaries that are non-negotiable.

If my beloved husband stands in the way of me reaching my highest potential, I will leave him. My [new] husband knows and understands this clearly. This is an example of a non-negotiable boundary. This was one of the boundaries I put in place before I raised my right hand for the second time.

Rules are not only necessary for the vitality of your marriage, but for every single relationship in which you enter. If you want your relationships to be healthy and thrive, you have got to set boundaries. If you think for a moment about the people you admire the most, you will realize that they have impenetrable boundaries established to ensure their health and well-being.

Your boss has boundaries. You wouldn't throw open the door to his office and scream at him. Your mother has boundaries. You wouldn't say vile curse words in front of her. And so it goes. You need boundaries.

Human beings need rules and institutions know that. This is why every time you step foot in an institution or a major organization they have a set of rules for you to follow. These organizations understand that if they don't give you their rules, you will inevitably create your own rules. That's just human nature. If we don't have rules we create our own rules. We not only create our own rules but we create rules that help us meet our objectives. We create rules that help us satisfy our own ego. It is human nature to live within boundaries, otherwise we have chaos and wrecked relationships. We also probably have no job, and certainly no friendships. We just don't often think about them in terms of ourselves.

My ex-husband did not know my rules (boundaries). It was never made clear to him that I'm not his possession and I can't be bullied. Because I did not tell him how to be with me, he made up his own rules. I was pissed, agitated, and angry but it was my own fault.

Now, let's think for a moment about all your failed, chaotic, or less-than-perfect relationships:

You and your Aunt Martha cannot get along.

Your mother constantly tells you how to clean your kitchen; it drives you crazy.

Your husband demands dinner at six o'clock every night and you hate that because you prefer to eat later.

Your children talk back to you and rarely show you the respect you deserve.

Who was the common denominator in every one of those relationships? Who shows up in each equation? YOU! You are the common denominator, just as I was the common denominator in all my failed relationships. We talked about this in Chapter 1. This might be a good time to go back and re-read that chapter.

You have to tell Aunt Molly and Uncle John how you want to be treated. If you don't tell don't tell Aunt Molly the rules, she will make up her own and then you'll get upset and say, "She should know better, she's a grown woman."

I agree with you; she should know better and the truth is, she does know better. But since she doesn't know your rules, she's left to make up her own, and let me warn you, the rules the people in your life make up will never be beneficial to you.

So, stop being lazy and start thinking about how you want your husband to treat you. But don't just tell your spouse how you want to be treated; teach your spouse how you should be treated. The way we treat ourselves is the way others treat us. Enter into a written agreement with your current spouse or any future spouses. Did I say written agreement? Yes, it needs to be in writing between you and your romantic partner.

It was two o'clock in the morning. I thought I heard the phone ringing. Could I be dreaming or was this real? The telephone rang and rang with a vengeance as I rolled on my side and tucked myself into a more comfortable position. Finally, I couldn't stand it any longer and I sat up.

I was angry at being awakened. My eyes were narrowed and rigid, my nostrils flaring. I was far gone on the angry train. I could not control the emotions that were balled up like a fist inside of me.

I snatched up the phone thinking: *Somebody better be dead!* But no, no one was dead. It was my mother calling because it was five o'clock in the morning Eastern Standard Time for her, and she was up having her coffee. It didn't occur to her that I was in California on PST and would be sound asleep. She thought it was the perfect time for us to have a nice long conversation about all the failures she had created in her life. She wanted to have her very own pity party and I was the guest who had to indulge her.

I could barely stand to listen to her as she proceeded to tell me about all her challenges. The more she talked the more my nostrils flared. By the end of the conversation, I was like a raging bull and my hand was a fist, ready to punch anyone in my path.

After I hung up the phone with her I took the alarm clock and threw it at the wall. Then I began sobbing. Life was getting a bit more complicated than I wanted it to be. Everyone was demanding something from me. My family, my boss, my extended family, and my coworkers. I was running on empty. My cup wasn't half full, it was completely empty. Little did I know giving from my empty cup was fueling my anger.

Today I understand that I was the cause of all my own pain and suffering because I had no boundaries in place. The panic attack that brought me to the emergency room that faithful morning was a result of not having boundaries. Everyone wanted and demanded something from me. I was clueless to the simple fact that I had to teach people how to treat me. But I could not teach anyone how to be in my space because I did not love and honor who I was. If you are serious about creating the life you desire, you better start loving who you are. Because only when you love yourself unconditionally, without judgement, can you set non-negotiable boundaries.

Abundance comes from being happy. It's really that simple. You cannot create freedom, joy, and abundance when you are unhappy. If you want more money to flood into your life, you have to live in the vibration of happiness. How can you be happy when everyone is pissing you off all day long? For years, I complained about how inconsiderate and selfish my mother was. I figured it was her job to figure out how to show up in my space.

No! How irresponsible of me to not say anything to my mother when she crossed the line. This wasn't the first time she had crossed the line. By the time I recognized I needed to set boundaries, it was too late. Our relationship had gone from average to dysfunctional.

Don't wait [like I did] until it's too late. Do your job and teach everyone who comes into your environment how to be with you. It's your job to stand up for yourself. No one will ever put boundaries in place for you. Stop complaining about how others treat you. Put your grownup pants on and start teaching the people in your life how you want to be treated.

By now you must be wondering: What are the benefits of having non-negotiable boundaries?

They allow you to make life decisions that serve and support you. You cannot make life decisions that support you if you don't have certain things in your life about which you are not willing to negotiate. With my ex-husband, it was nearly impossible for me to make major life decisions because he thought he owned me. Little did he know I cannot be bought or owned. I take full responsibility for that. When you set clear boundaries, you feel empowered. The feeling of being empowered allows you to take more control of your life. When you feel empowered, you make better choices.

If you are in a relationship with anyone and you don't feel empowered to make your own decisions, you are not with the right person. It doesn't matter if it's your friend or classmate, boss or spouse, aunt or mother, every human being on the planet should feel empowered in every single relationship into which they enter.

What are some of the things that you are not willing to negotiate? Think about that until you have a crystal clear idea what they are. You see, my dreams are not negotiable. I will not throw away my dreams and my drive simply to be married. I will not change who I am simply to be with someone. I will never put myself last on the list so that everyone else can be happy. That is a non-negotiable boundary for me. He knows it, and respects my boundaries. And by the way, I respect his boundaries as well. It's a two-way street, this boundary thing.

When I entered a partnership with my current husband, these terms and conditions were put in place and we both signed onto an agreement. I know what you are thinking: "That's going overboard, something in writing, we trust each other."

I'm going to tell you the truth; it is necessary. It's a must have. This is the only way you can hold yourself and your partner accountable.

If you find an excuse for not putting boundaries in place in your relationship, it's because you are getting something out of it. Now the question is: what are you getting out of it? I'll let you answer that question on your own. Why you would live like that is beyond my understanding.

But if you are ready to set boundaries, I'm proud of you and I'm excited for you because it's going to make your life a whole lot better. There are three important steps to take before you set your non-negotiable boundaries. The first step is to ask yourself these questions: What's important in any relationship? Is it respect? Is it communication? You need to ask yourself what your deal breakers are. The things you absolutely won't put up with. You need to know what they are. What are the things that make your nostrils flare? What are the things that make the hair on the back of your neck stand up? Unless you know what they are, you cannot set boundaries that are non-negotiable. Now, write them down. Make a list of your non-negotiable boundaries. Practice saying them aloud or in front of a mirror. Practice the conversation you are going to have with the individual with whom you plan to speak. The third step is to sit with the person and have the conversation. Make sure you are past the anger phase because if you are still angry with them, it's not going to go well.

The day I sat down to have a conversation about boundaries with my mother, it did not go well because I was too angry. When you come from a place of anger you shut down the lines of communication. When people sense anger, they put up defensive walls. Your words will not get through. Let them know you love and appreciate them and gently bring the way they have been treating you to their awareness. Let them know the new rules. You might want to say something like, "I'm sorry for not being strong enough to let you know that I don't like it when you treat me this way. I accept full responsibility for that but now I'm ready to honor myself. From now on I expect you to treat me like_____ (fill in the blank)." Whether it's correcting you in front of the children, or calling you at two o'clock in the morning, state your boundary. Be clear. But remember: It's not their fault, it's yours. You failed to be clear. Now you're being clear.

To recap, here are the three things you must do:

Make a list of your non-negotiable boundaries.

Write them down and practice saying them in front of a mirror.

Have the conversation.

The truth is, your relatives are not going to like the new set of rules. Especially if you have in-laws who are used to roaming through your space with no boundaries. Of course, some people will respect it and you will continue to have a meaningful relationship with them, but others will choose to walk out of your life because what they want out of the relationship they are no longer getting. You need to be okay with that. Make peace with it and move on. Remember that when you get better, better people enter your life. Be ready and open for the amazing people who are going to enter your space and support you on your journey. They will love you for your strong boundaries and admire your ability to set them. Clear boundaries help everyone in your life, especially you.

Chapter 5
Radical Completion: Finishing What You Start

Tuesday, January 12, 2010

I awoke from a dream that shook me to the core. In my dream, I was back in Haiti in my grandmother's house. Suddenly, violent shaking turned all hell loose upon our little home. I was overloaded with fear; no time to think. The ground was moving beneath us and the noise was like thunder with a violent shake coming from below. The big wall-sized portrait of my grandfather jumped off the wall as if it had a mind of its own. The dining room table flipped over. My feet felt heavy suddenly, like I was wearing lead boots. I became catatonic—voiceless, speechless—as my father raced through the house screaming and yelling for us to evacuate the house. One by one he got every single person out of the crumbling house. Yet I stood there wide-eyed, frozen with fear, as objects were being tossed all around me. Suddenly my father picked me up and carried me out of the house.

I woke up from the dream in a cold sweat and quickly picked up the phone to call my family in Haiti. I desperately needed to check on them. But after thinking the matter over, I hung up the phone and dismissed the dream as just another of my many nightmares. After all, it was not unusual for me to have them. I have been through so much trauma in my life, I have come to accept the fact that I'm supposed to have disturbing nightmares.

Later that day, as I was driving home from work, my phone started beeping nonstop. I got one text message after another—ding, ding, ding. The text messages came pouring in from everyone who knew I was a native-born Haitian. If took me a few minutes to realize something was not right. Who could this be? I pulled to the side of the road and that's when I learned there had just been an earthquake. A devastating, vicious 7.0 earthquake had struck Haiti!

Already a desperately poor nation, with little infrastructure and badly constructed buildings, this was probably one of the worst places on Earth for an earthquake to happen.

But it did. Acts of nature such as this have no concern for their victims. They strike without regard for humanity. The epicenter was near the town of Léogâne, approximately twenty-five kilometers west of Port-au-Prince, Haiti's capital. And very close to where my family lived.

I was shocked to say the least, but I was also numbed. I had a total of fifteen family members in Haiti, all living in the same neighborhood. It took great strength and effort to drive myself home that day and when I turned on the television I nearly fainted. The pain and the agony I felt that day was worse then the kidnapping I had experienced as a child. The pain was worse then the physical beatings I'd suffered at the hands of my brother. *How will I survive this? How will I go on after losing fifteen members of my tribal family?*

This was the exact same nightmare I'd had, except this news was true. The pain was real, the suffering was real. The anguish and screams that came out of me were real. It was more than my soul could bear. Unlike my dream, I could not just wake up, shower the nightmare away, and go on with my day.

I had learned to never ask why. That question was not allowed. My grandmother always told me, "If God puts it on your plate, that means you can handle it."

This time around, I wasn't sure if I *could* handle it. I asked God to show me the lesson; to help me understand the message that was being sent to me. There were no doubt lessons that my soul needed to learn, and I had no idea what they were.

I spent five days in bed without any food or fluids. My fight or flight mechanism kicked in and I lay in my bed for five days, unable to close my eyes. I felt helpless, and hopeless. I had survived many trials and tribulations, but I wasn't sure if I could survive this one.

I could hear and remember every single conversation I'd had with my grandmother. Her speeches were always in parables that as a child I did not understand, but as I got older the parables made sense to me.

The memories I shared with each of these individuals flashed like movie scenes clicking away in my mind. I had no ability to turn it off. Every single scene brought me to tears. Every single memory made the pain worse. I screamed aloud until my voice was gone and then I collapsed in my bed.

I was weak, empty, sad, and broken. What had once seemed important to me now had no meaning at all. Every single dream I'd had for my future no longer mattered. In this difficult moment, I realized I was nothing; however, I was too spiritually immature to understand that from *nothing* comes *everything*.

Six days after the earthquake, my cell phone rang. That thirty-second phone call changed everything. My father's girlfriend managed to call to let me know they were all alive! Wonderful news.

That phone call saved my life but it would be thirty more days before I heard anything else. But at least I knew they were alive; it would be another two weeks before I stopped lighting candles for them.

During this difficult time in my life, I had been at odds with my mother. We have actually never gotten along. My earliest memory of my mother was a blow I received from her that knocked out my two front teeth. I grew up physically, but the bloody-mouthed little girl inside me never grew up. My mother and I had not spoken for the last year and now she was blowing up my phone checking to see if I had received any news. I could not pick up the phone to talk to her or deal with her. I was in too much pain and my mother was the last person I wanted to speak with. It was at that moment, I realized I needed help. I needed to address all the issues around my mother that were sitting on my 'someday' shelf.

How many issues do you have sitting on your 'someday' shelf? How many people do you need to forgive? What childhood issues do you need to let go of?

As children, we are taught to complete our work. If you had the type of grandmother I had, you never left anything incomplete. Most of us have been lectured about finishing what we start.

When we become adults, however, we leave a lot of things incomplete and unfinished. We tell ourselves, "I'm a grown up. I can decide."

Perhaps you started a degree you never completed. I'm not sure what you have or have not completed in your life, but one thing I'm certain of is that you have left a lot of core issues in your life incomplete. We all have; you're certainly not alone or unique in that regard.

If you are depressed, I'm sure you have not taken the time to address the real causal issues of your depression, or the real cause of your anxiety or panic attacks. Have you ever wondered why you just can't seem to get to the next level of your greatness? Why is it that your genius never shows up? It's because you have never take the time to "be complete" with the people and situations that no longer serve you.

What does it mean to be complete? Simply put, it means to make peace with the situation. Finish it. Don't leave things hanging or sitting on the shelf mocking you.

Until you make peace—come to a resolution —with the situation or relationship, you cannot move past it.

Completion is not simply saying, "I'm done with this." Relationships, not just tasks and projects, need to be completed. You cannot just avoid the issues you have with your partner, parents, friends, co-workers, or even your boss. The core issues need to be addressed. Until you address them and become complete with them (arrive at a resolution), you will never be able to reach your next level of success or greatness. Freedom, joy, and abundance cannot find you if you are surrounded by bits and pieces of trauma, broken relationships, incomplete tasks, and unfinished drama.

Are you in a relationship with someone who, when a discussion gets heated, just walks away? Does that ever solve anything? Sure, it eases the tension for a while, and lets everyone calm down. But nothing is resolved by walking away.

In order to obtain financial freedom, you have to become complete with debt. If you want to stop dieting, you have to be complete with being overweight. Completion means you are ready to put it away, be at peace with it, and write the next chapter of your life.

You need to become complete with the things you no longer desire to have in your life, and be free to create the things you do desire. You need to become complete with every single failure. I recently heard someone say "honor your scar tissue" and understand that your scars are proof that you survived whatever caused the injury. A scar is evidence of healing. But if you still have open wounds, then they need to be allowed (or forced) to heal. The decision is yours.

Why is it important to be complete with the failures? Because if you are not complete with failing, you can't start creating success. Failure is the reciprocal of success. What do you get out of completion? There are four major benefits to completion.

The first benefit is that *completion opens the door to forgiveness.* To create freedom, joy, and abundance you have to forgive the people who have hurt you. Without forgiveness, you cannot start a new chapter. A lack of forgiveness keeps you in the past and the future is not created in the past. For many years, I searched for my calling. I knew I was here to do something more than just be a Registered Nurse (although that is an awesome profession) but I could not for the life in me figure out what that "something more" was. It wasn't until I made a choice to complete my relationship with my mother that I was finally able to find my higher calling. If you are wondering what's next for you, or why you can't produce the success you desire in your life or business, it's time for you to take a look at what you have on your someday shelf.

The second reason completion is important is that it helps you move past the situation. Being complete is what allows you to move past the pain, anger, or resentment. You cannot move past the pain until you've made good with the situation. You will continue to hate your mom, dad, ex-husband, or boss until you make a conscious choice to end that chapter.

The third reason completion is important is that it allows you to create something new. When you are complete with financial struggles, you create abundance in your life. When you are complete with failed relationships, you can create relationships that are more meaningful.

The fourth reason completion is important is because completion releases you from negative energy. When you become complete about the relationships that did not work, you are able to move away from the negative energy of the relationship. You no longer invest any emotions as to what your ex-husband [for example] is doing.

I spent many years being angry at my mother for what she did or didn't do (to me). I did not yet understand that my mother was a great teacher and she was there to teach me things I did not know. The abuse and neglect I suffered at my mother's hands made me the mother I am today.

Listen, I've been there. And I want you to understand that your pain, suffering, and struggles are there to strengthen you. You do not become strong by having an easy path! The challenges are there to make you better than you were before. To live a life where you are free to travel the world, do work that you love, and have plenty of money to spend on the things you desire, you have to become complete with every single situation in your life.

I can hear you now, arguing with that voice in your head. You know, the voice that really isn't your friend. The one that's saying, "I can never forgive my ex-husband. Girl, you have no idea what that man put me through! And what does she mean by completion anyway. I'm not understanding the whole completion thing."

Okay, let me make it simple for you: Just get over yourself! Take a good look at yourself, and stop focusing on your ex. I spent many years blaming my mother and being upset with her as if I was the perfect daughter with no blame. None of us are perfect; we are all human beings who entered this journey called life without a guide book. The mistakes you are making are your guide book. As you learn and grow from those mistakes, you will move away from the things you no longer desire to create, to the things you do want.

There's a five-step process to completion and if you faithfully and honestly follow these steps, I promise you will be able to turn the vision in your head to a reality. Here they are:

Step 1: *Pull the unfinished "on hold" issues off the shelf.* Deal with the issue. When I first started making decent money, I just spent it all. I lived paycheck to paycheck, never saving a dime. I never balanced my check book. A few years later, I looked at my tax return from the previous year. I had made $150K that year and, I had not a dime to my name. It was shocking. Where had my money gone? I realized my "unfinished and incomplete" issue was learning how to handle my money.

The issue turned out to be how I actually felt about money. My tribal family had always been broke and stuck in poverty. Turns out I felt guilty for having money so I gave them some and spent the rest to get rid of the guilt. No money, I thought, no guilt. "I'm broke just like you." That turned out to be the wrong thinking and once I saw clearly that I was letting my tribal family drag me down with them, I changed my money-handling strategy. By putting my financial security first on my list, I was actually to help others even more. But who I helped, and when and how, was up to me. They were not driving the Naomi Train. I was in charge.

So, what's the real issue that's keeping you from creating the life you desire? If it's not money, what's the real issue that's keeping you from finding a relationship that supports you in your journey? What's the real issue that makes you spend every dime? What do you do once you identify the issue? Once you discover the core issue, it's time to deal with it. It's time to embrace the mirror.

Step 2: *Don't numb the pain!* Not with alcohol, drugs, promiscuous sex, or food. The obesity issue we are having in America today is in direct correlation to numbing the pain. The alcohol you are putting in your body to help you forget is not going to help you. You cannot and should not numb the pain. You are here to feel pain. Feeling pain is the process in which you grow. The greater the pain, the more growth you experience. That anguished pain I felt when I thought I'd lost fifteen members of my family brought tremendous growth in my life. If I had chosen to numb my pain with alcohol, I would be an alcoholic and the pain will still be there. But today I get an opportunity to share with you and help you on your journey of creating the life you desire to live. I want you to know though you are here to feel pain, you are not here to suffer. Suffering is not the same as feeling pain. Suffering is an unconscious choice that people make. It is not God's will for you to suffer. The pain I felt of not having a single dime to my name forced me to change my mindset and my habits around money.

Step 3: *Make the decision to be complete.* Everything starts with a decision-a deliberate choice. Decide to stop struggling financially. Decide to stop dating men who cannot support your vision for the future. Make a decision to stop eating just because it feels good. Until you decide, you cannot take the next step.

Step 4: *Let go of the situation.* You have to let go. I had to let go of my issues around guilt or feeling like I did not deserve the life I had.

Step 5: *Learn the lessons.* Every single event in your life or situation you encounter brings a specific lesson you need to learn. Don't ask 'why me?' Ask 'what is the lesson I need to learn?' Until you learn the lesson, you cannot move past the situation. I had to personally learn all the lessons in all the failed relationships in my life in order for me to find the man that is capable of supporting me on my journey. Often, the lessons won't come until you've made a choice to be complete.

Let me share another story with you. One hot summer day after not seeing my grandmother for many years, my younger sister called to tell me that she was at my mother's house. It was a Saturday afternoon and I had a break in my schedule. My grandmother had always been a very sarcastic woman. She's also a tiny little person, no more than four foot eleven, but what she lacked in height she made up for in tall character. Unlike the rest of the young adults in my tribal family, I loved to spend time with her, even though the parables she spoke made no sense to me. There was something about those parables that I loved. Perhaps my soul knew I would someday not have access to her and would need her words of wisdom. On this particular day, I arrived at my mother's house in a depressed and anxious state.

I had been in an intimate relationship for many years. The relationship was stagnant, to say the least. I knew there was no future for us but something was keeping me with this man. I found my grandmother sitting at the kitchen table waiting for my arrival. I sat next to her and began a conversation around my life. My grandmother listened as I talked my head off, dumping all my problems on her. She sat patiently and listened to me. I honestly expected her to give me a sermon. I expected her to do the same thing the rest of my tribal family always did. I expected her to tell me how stupid I was. I expected her to be angry and disappointed with me. But she wasn't. She said, "My dear child, there's a price for everything."

What? That made no sense to me. I had no idea what she was talking about. Even when I asked her to explain she would laugh and say, "One day you will come to know."

And I always answered, "Come to know what?" But she never elaborated. I drove myself home later that evening thinking about the conversation I'd had with her. The phrase 'there's a price for everything' played in my mind over and over.

Today I have come to understand the point my grandmother was driving home. Yes, there's a price for everything. The stagnant relationship I was in had been over for a year, I had just refused to exit. I had adopted a wait and see approach, and not just in that relationship, but in others as well. All that 'waiting and seeing' caused confusion. *Should I leave Florida? Should I move to Georgia? What should I do with my life?*

What I did not understand at the time, was that the failure to be *complete with a relationship* that no longer served me, kept me from being clear on what was next in my life. It was like being stuck in the mud. Only when you pull yourself out of the mud, can you move forward. When you are incomplete you lack clarity. Clarity is power and without clarity you have no power to achieve anything. Without clarity, you cannot create a new future.

When you make the decision to stay incomplete, you get to keep the pain, and the resentment, and the hurt of the past. When you decide to stay incomplete you make a decision to have the things you desire not show up in your life. You get robbed of the things that are important to you because you focus all your energy on the things you are incomplete about. Being incomplete is what's keeping you from finding your life's path and purpose. If you don't choose to be complete, you are choosing to stay in the same spot.

Today, right now, I urge you to be complete with every single relationship that is not working for you. I urge you to become complete with every single situation in your life that is less than desirable. Completion will set you free from the shackles around your ankles. The shackles that keep you from moving forward. Completion is the key to creating a life of freedom, joy, and abundance. No, it isn't easy to make peace with the past, but it's necessary to create the future. Get unstuck. Pull yourself out of the mud pit, and move forward!

Chapter 6
The Awakened Spirit

January 1, 2005

It was the beginning of a brand-new year, usually an exciting day for me, filled with hope and promise. But time I went through the most difficult moment of my life. Even to this day, so many years later, I still consider it so.

My father was being deported after spending twenty-three years in prison for second-degree murder. He had gone to prison three months after I entered the United States. Indeed, life was hard for my mother, who had depended on my father for every single need. She was a helpless infant wrapped in an adult body. She could not take care of her own basic needs, never mind the needs of the three children she was left to care for. So, I had to step in and be the adult, taking care of my mother and her other two children. When you are nine years old and you've been handed such a huge responsibility, you make a lot of mistakes.

Today I've come to the understand they weren't mistakes at all. The universe was preparing me for the life I have today.

I worked very hard to escape the poverty into which I had taken up my incarnation. I made good with it when I enrolled myself in nursing school and became a Registered Nurse. The young spirit that lacks experience is unaware that there is no destination in life, but rather life is a journey unfolding every second of every day. I felt I had achieved all my goals. I thought I should be happy given that I had escaped teenage pregnancy, not been addicted to drugs, and had dropped all the baggage that usually comes with being raised in Little Haiti.

That neighborhood, Little Haiti, was once featured on the news magazine show *60 Minutes*, describing it as one of the poorest neighborhoods in the country. But at that point in my life, I wasn't poor at all. I was living the American dream, yet something was missing; I could not figure out what was wrong with me. At the same time my father was being deported, hurricane Katrina slammed into the Gulf Coast. It so happened that my uncle, his wife, and his four children were all affected by the storm. Though everyone survived, the stress of it all was enough to send me into a major depression. I wondered if our family was blighted.

I no longer knew who I was. It seemed as if I had changed overnight. What was important to me was no longer important. I had taken the vacations I wanted. I had experienced what it was like to be able to do the things I'd dreamed of doing. The universe had fulfilled everything on my wish list. But I was not happy; I was depressed.

The question was: Now what? What do you do when all your dreams have been turned into reality. Most people spend their entire life chasing after their dreams, but there I was at the tender age of thirty-one and I had lived out all the dreams of my youth. I turned to the self-help gurus for the answer. They all told me to get another dream. That was easier said than done. I had no other dreams. The journey from poverty to middle class had taken the wind out of my sails. The thought of finding another dream made me sick to my stomach and all the emotional baggage I placed on the 'someday shelf' brought more distress in my life. No one ever bothered to tell me that I was mind, body, and spirit and of the three, the spirit was the greatest.

On the journey to make something out of my life, I had neglected my spirit. I was dead on the inside but on the outside, it looked like I had everything. Most nights I cried myself to sleep wondering if this was going to be where the road ended for me. There had to be more. My soul was longing for something bigger. I could not fulfill that need at the time; I did not understand the conscious and subconscious mind. I was unaware of the subconscious mind and the ability it has to solve every single problem in my life. If you desire to be more and have more in your life, understand the functions of these two minds.

Let me introduce you to the conscious mind; the mind you use every single day. This mind is responsible for short-term memory, planning, will power, and critical thinking. I understood this mind because it was the mind that I used to create the freedom, and the abundance, I was experiencing. I planned my life meticulously, taking control of every single detail, without leaving anything to chance. My will was strong and I used my will power to move me past my blocks.

Though I understood the conscious mind, I had no clue what the subconscious mind was all about. What is this mind and how does it affect your ability to create massive wealth, freedom, and joy? Let me make the introductions!

After many nights crying myself to sleep, curled up in a ball, I decided one day that it was time to take action. I have always been good at taking action. If there's a problem, I'm going to find a solution.

I began to think about a conversation I'd once had with my grandmother; the woman of many parables. The woman who gave me advice that I was incapable of understanding. When we had that conversation, I was overweight, bankrupt, and my relationships were a disaster. "Why is life so hard?" I asked my grandmother.

She looked at me, her eyes locked with mine, and she said, "Because you don't ask."

Who was I supposed to ask? What was I supposed to ask them? It never occurred to me that someone else knew the answers to the things I did not know.

Now, you need to know that I grew up in the church because my grandmother was a believer. Once a former Voodoo worshipper, she had found the Christian God. She taught everyone about the God she had come to love. I learned about God and knew of Jesus Christ, the son of God. I had, in fact, meet Jesus when I had a near-death experience shortly after my eighth birthday.

During that meeting, Jesus had revealed a lot of truth to me but that truth would coil dormant inside of me until I was ready to find it. The truth I bottled inside was like a precious jewel I stored, not wanting anyone to steal it from me. By the time I was sixteen years old, I was complete with the church, because nothing I had learned in my near-death experience came close to what the

Baptist Church was preaching. (I will share this truth with you in my next book!) My tribal family saw me as being disobedient and they weren't afraid to let me know that God's anger would fall upon my head for leaving the church. The God that was being presented to me was not the God I encountered during my journey to the other side.

The church kept me in constant confusion. The Baptist Church taught pain, suffering, and that it was all a part of God's plan. The rich will never make it to Heaven as they have been handed their wealth here on this plane; however, the poor had favor in God's eyes. "Read your scripture and pray and God will take care of the rest," they said.

By the time I was eleven years old, I had come to my own conclusion: God would not take care of it. The woman that was living inside of the eleven-year-old child's body had to roll up her sleeves and make things happen. After several fights and arguments with my aunts, uncles, and the rest of the tribe, I retired from church in order to search out my own truth.

When I left the church, I forgot about the spirit. I forgot that I was one with this energy. I did not have the recollection that this energy lives inside of me and that I was part of God. I in my own right had the capability of creating what I wanted and how I wanted it. I did not have the knowledge that I was a master and I could reinvent my life. I was not aware that in order to find a new dream I would have to connect with the subconscious mind. To find my way out of deep depression, I would have to get in touch with the mind that knows all there is to know. To buy my freedom from working the long horrible nursing hours, I would need to ask this mind for direction. This hidden mind held all the answers to the questions I had. Questions like why was I so unhappy at my career. After all, it was the career I had chosen and worked hard to be good at. Why had I escaped the poverty but the rest of my family continued to struggle? Was I better than them? It was in my moment of quest that I discovered the subconscious mind.

In chapter three I introduced you to the subconscious mind. It's vital that you come to understand this mind if you are sincere about transforming your life. Once again, let me introduce you to the subconscious mind. The subconscious mind is the mind is where your spirit lives. It is responsible for your habits and patterns; the way you show up in the world. The subconscious mind stores your long-term memory, cellular memory, emotions, and creativity. Your conscious mind houses your will power; however, the subconscious mind is where your true power and potential are stored.

To design the life you desire, it's imperative to get in touch with your true source of power. I'm not pushing my beliefs on you, but there is an energy that lives within all of us. If you dare tap into this energy, you will find your genius.

I call this energy God but you can call it whatever you choose. Tree, mushroom, Vishnu…whatever you choose…it doesn't matter, just know and understand that this energy lives within you and its power and abilities are stored in the subconscious part of your brain. That's just true, as true as I can convey to you, regardless of what you call it. It's like having a secret power outlet in your home. You ignore it for years, then you discover this hidden power source and you plug into it. Wow! All of a sudden, your world lights up like the Las Vegas Strip.

The conscious mind knows right from wrong but it doesn't always do what's right. For example, consciously you may know that it's not good to spend money you don't have. But for some reason you ignore this fact and you pull out your credit card and spend money you don't have. More and more Americans are in debt because their subconscious mind is not on board with the plan to get out of debt. If you want to create freedom, joy, and abundance in your life, it's important for you to get the subconscious mind on board. It's not enough for the conscious mind to know something. The subconscious mind needs to know it as well. If the subconscious mind is not on board you will repeat your old patterns and you will fail over and over again. Have you ever met someone who can't seem to catch a break? Life is hard for them. Everything they do works against them. In religion, they say the adversary [or the Devil] is busy.

I stated in previous chapters that there is no force working against you. The result you produce in the world is in direct correlation to how much you have tapped into the subconscious mind. This energy is the light that illuminates the world. If you are poor, it's because you are not connected to this power source. If you are middle class, it's because you have a bit more connection to the source. And those who are wealthy have plugged directly into this source of energy. If you want more money, you have to raise your vibration and connect with the divine that lives within you.

I just made that sound simple, right? Did you go looking around your house for a magical power outlet? I hope not! Because it's not as simple as it first seems, but neither is it impossible. Let's dig a little deeper.

The subconscious mind can work for you or against you. It's all up to you. When you are walking through life half asleep and unaware, the subconscious mind usually works against you, often by just being idle. Your job is to awaken this mind and make sure it is working for you. The subconscious mind knows itself and doesn't need praise or glory; it is quiet power; it's capable of everything, therefore, there's no need to announce it. It stays asleep until the moment you call on it. When you call on this mind, it comes quickly and brings its power to help you climb the mountains in your life. But this mind will not force you to come to know to it. The subconscious mind is your secret super power!

We all have been given the freedom of choice. You are free to choose how your want to live your life. You are free to choose your sexual orientation. You are free to choose your morals and your beliefs. And you are free to choose whether or not you want to work with your subconscious mind. But the moment you decide to work with this mind, your life will be transformed. You will not recognize who you are, nor will you remember who you were before.

Planning comes from your *conscious* mind. You know that you should plan for retirement but you don't. Why don't you plan for retirement? Because the subconscious mind is clueless as to what needs to be done. It's sleeping and hasn't been put to work. To design your best life, you have got to get these two minds on the same track. They have to work together, like a pair of draft horses pulling the wagon, instead of one pulling and the other sleeping. To design your life the way you want it to be, you must have a deeper understanding of the subconscious mind and how to get it on board.   Earl Nightingale said, *"Whatever [seeds] you plant in your subconscious mind, and nourish with repetition and emotion, will one day become a reality."*

Pay attention to the words *nourish and repetition.* Why do you think Earl uses those words? He uses them for two reasons: The subconscious mind will run wild unless you nourish it with the right food, which is information. To get the subconscious mind on board, you have to tell this mind over and over again what needs to be done. Otherwise it will continue to doze and not get the message. Your alarm clock tools are REPITITION and AFFIRMATION.

Here's an example: You don't feel like you are worthy of love. So to change that mindset, every morning and before bed at night, you say aloud, "I deserve to be loved." Say it twenty-one times. Remember, repetition. The sleeping subconscious mind will eventually get the message and you will begin to see yourself as worthy of being loved. And when you see yourself in such a positive light, others will too. That's how the subconscious mind helps you accomplish your goals. Tell it again and again to help you pull that wagon. Giddy up, brain!

I feel a story coming on! So, one Saturday morning I woke up and the street was filled with children my age. I looked out the window at a street filled with ten- and eleven-year-old inner-city kids; a loud and busy street. Everyone seemed to be having a grand old time. Many of the girls jumped roped and played double Dutch. Their pigtails seemed to be jumping with them. Their faces were filled with joy. They were all clueless as to how poor they were, but not me. I was always way too aware of my condition and jumping rope in the street with kids my age was of no interest to me. After all, I was a grown woman stuck in a child's body. I asked my mother to give me thirty-five cents to catch the bus. This particular morning, I wanted to catch the bus and stroll through Miami Shores.

Miami Shores, according to my family, was where the rich people lived. I wanted to know who these rich people were. Perhaps if I took a hard look at them I would find something different in them and maybe I could figure out why God made them so special and gave them all the wealth. I got off the bus and proceeded to walk several blocks before I entered the well-manicured neighborhood of Miami Shores. My chest was pounding, my heart racing like a race car. I was terrified someone was going to call the police and report me; for sure I had no business as a poor girl walking these streets of (in my mind) gold.

I walked up and down the street looking at one big beautiful house after another. An old white lady who was about eighty-five years old was sitting on her front porch. She was surprised to see me in her neighborhood. Was I lost? Was I the child of a housekeeper working in one of the big houses?

As I walked past her front porch, I felt a sense of discomfort and the feeling of inferiority. "Good morning, young lady," she called out to me. Suddenly my throat had something caught in it. I was choking on my own saliva. I could not believe she was addressing me. Me the little black girl from the inner city who had more self esteem issues than anyone you will ever meet.

She persisted, "What has brought you to this neck of the woods?"

Again, I opened mouth to reply but nothing came out. I had been struck dumb.

She just smiled. "It's okay. I just want to make sure you are not lost."

At that point, despite her soft voice, I was terrified she was going to call the police. I managed to squeak out, "No, ma'am, I'm not lost. I'm from Little Haiti and I just wanted to see where the rich people live."

"Well, then, you are in the wrong neighborhood, child! We are not rich here.

We are simply middle class."

Middle class? What was that? My thoughts were about rich and poor. Was there a middle? I had no idea what she was talking about but whatever this neighborhood was, it was definitely a better class than where I lived.

Amazingly, she invited me inside. I was shocked but too scared to say no. So in I went, and found her house to be beautiful, decorated with antiques, which she said was just a bunch of old furniture.

She was lonely and I was lonely. We both needed a friend and she asked me if I wanted to have lunch with her. I helped her make a sandwich and we each ate half. She said it was nice to have someone to eat with. "You can have anything you want, little Gina," she said, "even a house bigger than this one. Don't ever let anyone tell you different."

Of course, I didn't believe her but it sounded nice. She shared stories about her life and her family. They were all dead or had moved away, she told me, a sad look on her wrinkled face. I felt blessed to be in her company. She invited me to come and spend Saturdays with her anytime I wanted to. And I took her up on it, whenever I could scrape together the thirty cents for the bus fare.

One day as we sat on her porch, I declared that this was where I wanted to live. Though I wasn't sure how it was going to happen, I began to nourish this thought. I visualized it and I gave thanks to it every single day. It wasn't an easy thing to do because the ego would constantly remind me of what I did not have. Today I live in a much bigger, grander house than that dear lady did, as I somehow knew I had to nourish that seed she'd helped me plant in my subconscious mind.

How many times have you decided to take a step forward in your life and there stands your ego, telling you what's possible and what's not possible. How do you handle your ego when it shows up? I had to learn to talk back to my ego.

The ego loves to be comfortable and with any possible sign of change, the ego goes into freak-out mode. How are you going to get out of this one? The ego: "You won't be able to find another husband. You have two children, nobody wants someone with children. You have way too much baggage." And this goes on and on. It will continue to go on until you make the choice to stop the negative conversations in your head. You must talk back to your ego. Thank your ego for protecting you. It's only doing its job. Your ego lives based on fear but your spirit lives based on possibility.

Your ego will go to great lengths to protect you but it is your job to let the ego know that it's okay for you to move to the next chapter of your life. It's your job to let your ego know that this season of your life is over and you are ready for the next season. Though I was not aware of it, I had tapped into my subconscious mind and said 'get out of the inner city'. The subconscious mind is a problem solver. It will solve every single problem you encounter. How the heck was I going to leave the inner city? The more I pounded, the more I began to find that little speck of light. One day the answer as to how I would make my escape out of the inner city came to me in a flash like lightning.

Learning came easy to me. As a matter of fact, learning was my first love. As far back as I can remember, I wanted to know things. To this day, learning remains my first love. Because I love to learn, I was good in school. Reading and writing were the tools I used to escape the abuse in my home.

One day after a huge argument with my mother, I was laying face down on my bed crying my heart out. Suddenly a voice from nowhere spoke to me. I didn't hear the voice in my head; I heard it in my heart. The voice was calm and very sure of itself, when it said, "You can get out of here if you want to." *Wow! I could do that!*

I meditated on this for days. This mind—this voice that I had no idea where it came from —knew exactly how to solve my problem. When Monday morning finally arrived, I ran to my guidance counselor's office and eagerly introduced myself to her. I told her about my plan to go to college. She said she couldn't help me because I was only a sophomore. It would be two more years before she could be of any use to me. But her discouragement didn't phase me. Every single day I poked my head into her office to remind her about my dream, and I even had lunch with her a couple times a week. I became that student she just could not get rid of and at the end of my junior year, she helped me get a writing scholarship that paid for the first two years of my college education. By that time, I think she would have almost paid for it herself to get me off her back!

I share this story with you so you can see the power of the subconscious mind. The subconscious mind is the mind that thinks. Only when you make time to think about your challenges, will you find the answer. The answers you are looking for are not on social media. You have to tap into the power source within yourself to find the answers. *Seek and ye shall find.* If you are not finding the people who are capable of helping you on your journey, it's because you are not seeking. *Ask and it shall be given unto you.*

If you don't have what you desire, it's because you are not asking.

When you think of this mind, you need to think of it as the soil in which you plant the seed of whatever you want to grow. The desire to have freedom, joy, and abundance is the seed to manifest freedom, joy, and abundance. The desire to share your life with someone who will cherish you and allow you to be your authentic self, is the seed to grow your reality.

But—here's the truth—you need to be the one who plants the seed. The subconscious mind is where you need to plant the seed of your desire, as it knows exactly how to make it your reality. No one else can plant the seed for you.

What do you want to create? Whatever it is, go right ahead and ask the subconscious mind. You don't need to conduct a sermon and long convoluted prayers. What's needed to work with this mind is your ability to trust and act, despite your fears.

Getting your subconscious mind on board is a three-step process:

Step One: S*top doing and start thinking.* If you are not finding the relationship that is right for you, stop looking for it and start thinking. Start asking the right questions. Ask the questions that empower you. If you can't find the opportunities that will help you in your journey to creating freedom, joy, and abundance, then stop looking for opportunities and start listening. When you stop frantically doing, you are able to listen and receive the guidance you need to get you where you desire to be. You know the people who always seem to be at the right place at the right time? It's because they think and they listen. That is the way to awaken your subconscious mind.

Step Two: *Let go of security and become comfortable with uncertainty.* Clinging to security is like standing still in quicksand! Everyone is looking for security. The endless search for security has caused the human race to live lives that don't belong to them. When your primary focus is security, you get stuck working in a career that is not for your highest good. You find yourself staying in romantic relationships that do not support you in your journey. Stop looking for security and start believing in the endless possibility within you, just waiting to be cultivated.

Step Three: *Carve out time to get to know the subconscious mind.* In today's world, being frantically busy has become the norm. You are running along in the race, keeping up with people on social media. You are busy trying to plan life as you think it should happen. Take fifteen minutes a day and you can transform your life. In fifteen minutes a day you can stop running and connect with your true essence; connect [plug in] to all the power that is within you. I can tell you about this energy, this force, and this storehouse of endless wealth, but only you can tap into it. You are the only person who can do the work. I cannot do the work for you. My hope is that after reading this book, you will find the inspiration to love yourself enough to stand up for who you were meant to be.

Chapter 7
Play the Money Game, Not Your Ego's Game

My business coach, a powerful woman and successful executive, whom I adore and wholeheartedly admire, invited me to attend a seminar designed to help speakers and writers step up their game.

I was skeptical, to say the least, when she said, "Naomi, are you coming to *Speak and Write to Make Millions*?"

Oh, believe me, I wanted to make millions. That sounded awesome. But still...I wondered...me?

She persisted: "Oh, you have to come to Speak & Write so you can understand what I'm asking you to do."

I said: "Oh, okay..." What I really meant was "Don't count on it!" It was the kind of "okay" that means "thank you for sharing but I'm not interested."

You see, in reality I had no plans to attend a seminar. I was way too busy with my life; taking care of my son, and a thousand other things. And now this woman was asking me to pay for a seminar, fly to San Diego, and (oh…it gets better) I would have to pay for my own hotel and meals.

Are you kidding me? The conversation in my head went something like this: "Look, Mrs. Executive Coach, I don't make the kind of money you make. I have a five-year-old son who wants Batman and Batgirl at his birthday party and I have to pay for that, and super-heroes don't come cheap. My husband is working too, so I have to figure out who's going to watch my son if I leave town; probably hire someone because we don't have the luxury of nearby family. My reasons for not going were unending.

And you know what Sybil (my alter ego) said? She sarcastically sneered, "Sure, coach, I'll just drop everything I'm doing and come to your *Speak and Write* seminar. No problem."

How many times have you had that same type of conversation in your head? You see, I had even forgotten about the 'make a million' part, even though I very much wanted to make millions doing what I love. What I heard in my head, though, were the excuses as to why I could not go. I bet you recognize that negative talk, as something that invades your mind too, right?

Let me quickly say that I have been fortunate to have been coached a lot during my life. Coaching is something I value and appreciate; it's smart to take advantage of others' experience and knowledge to build up where you are weak.

So now when my mind wants to do what it wants to do, thanks to the thousands of dollars spent on coaching fees, I can catch myself. So, in that very moment, I had to say to my ego, "Thank you for sharing, but I'm choosing to play the money game and not the ego game."

If you want to create freedom, joy, and abundance in your life, you have to stop playing the ego game and play the money game. The moment you start complaining and making excuses about the things you cannot do to move you forward in your business, relationships, or career, you are playing the ego game.

I recognized that the conversation in my head was a result of my own ego. My ego was too comfortable playing a game that will keep me from moving forward in my journey of being an entrepreneur. My ego was ready to play its own game and not the money game that would allow me to create the two million dollars I said I was going to create.

Your ego is no different then mine. The ego loves comfort and the ego is a master at helping you play your own ego game so that changes don't take place. Next thing you know, it's been five years since you started trying to get out of debt. Your ego even tells you that you've done your best, but the reality is you have more debt now then you did five years ago. It's also been eight years since you began looking for Mr. Right and he's still in hiding. Now you are convinced

it's not going to happen. Your ego works hard to keep you exactly where you are.
It's very clever, your ego. It will give you a quick script.

The script goes something like this:

"It's never going to happen for me. I'm turning forty this year."

You say it as if forty is ancient. If you think forty is too old to find the person with whom you want to share the rest of your life, wait until you turn eighty and are alone. If you think forty is too late to start saving and planning for retirement, wait 'till you are seventy-five and still working. You don't want that, right? To be eighty, alone and still working?

I had to put my ego aside and play the money game that was in front of me. I did everything I need to do, and took the trip; San Diego opened many doors for me. To play the money game, you need to find your 'why'? Why do you want to share your life with someone? Why do you want to travel the world? Why do you want to quit your job and pursue your dreams? Your 'why' needs to be crystal clear or you will continue to play the wrong game. I had to take a strong look at my 'why'. I'm passionate about sharing my message with the world. I'm passionate about leaving a legacy behind for my son and my future grandchildren. I'm passionate about transforming the lives of women all across the globe. Knowing my 'why' helped me stop playing my ego game and play the money game.

As I Ubered my way from San Diego International Airport to the beautiful hotel where the *Speak and Write* event was being held, I felt proud of myself. I felt proud that I did not allow my ego to let me play my own game. The event was amazing. It really blew me away and gave me so many good nuggets of wisdom that I can apply to my business and personal life.

My business coach is an amazing speaker. She had the crowd rolling with laughter when she picked up a chair and dragged it behind her to demonstrate how we were all dragging our baggage behind us, complaining and refusing to take radical action to transform our lives. She was on fire and she had the crowd on fire. Passion is as catching as the spark of an ember touching dry tinder.

Men and women were clapping, laughing, and shouting. The energy in the room was that of fierce warriors. A tall woman with skin the color of dark chocolate, stood up and yelled, "Preach it!" She was on fire and she let her excitement flow. It was amazing.

Then the speaker made an offer to the excited crowd. She offered these women an opportunity to work with her one on one. I expected the entire room to run and sign up with her but only a handful of women— those truly hungry for change in their lives and businesses—joined her on stage. I was one of them! In fact, I ran so I wouldn't be left out!

I was happy and excited for us; these women who scrambled up on stage, ready to change our lives. The others probably didn't know it yet, but I knew we had all made a decision that would change our lives forever.

Lunchtime rolled around and I went out to lunch with the group of women who had signed up for the executive coaching program.

They were excited and could not wait to get back for the second half of the presentation. I was too hungry to care about getting back on time, so I stayed and finished my lunch. Hey, a girl's gotta eat!

A young woman in her mid-thirties approached my table. "Is anyone sitting here?"

I looked up and I saw her staring at my name tag. She was wearing the same name tag from the event. The women of that community call themselves unicorns because they have dreams that no one else understands. It's very easy for one unicorn to spot another.

I signaled her to the empty seat across from me. She sat down and we started having the same conversation every pair of strangers has. "Where are you from?" "How are you liking the event?"

Moments later she warmed up to me and began to share her dreams of building a multimillion-dollar company in the health and fitness industry. Throughout the conversation she could not stop taking about my business coach. I thought it would help her if I shared that the funny, confident, and powerful women she saw on stage could deliver a five-hundred percent increase in her business. I proceeded to tell her that the woman she admired is my business coach.

"How is it working with her?" She excitingly asked.

I told her all about my wonderful experiences. She was excited to hear all I had to share about my mentor and then suddenly she asked, "How much does she charge?"

With a huge smile on my face, I said, "Her fee is twenty-five thousand for ten sessions."

Her jaw dropped. She leaned back in her seat while locking her eyes on mine. Clearly, she thought I was either lying or insane. At that moment, the waiter walked by with his water pitcher in hand. He sensed that he had interrupted an intense conversation and quickly made his exit. "I'll come be back later," he said.

As she stared at me, I could almost hear the conversation going on in her head:

"Are you crazy?"

"Why would you pay her that kind of money?"

"And where did you get that kind of money? Are you a drug dealer? A prostitute? A bank robber?"

I just watched her silently as she wrestled with her own ego. After what seemed to be a lifetime of silence between us she said, "I could never do that."

In a calm voice I said, "Of course not."

She instantly became defensive and her sassy black-woman attitude came to the surface, her internal arguments lost for the moment. "Why you said it like that?"

I said, giving her attitude right back, "Because you are not willing to play to win. You are too busy playing your ego game."

She rolled her eyes. If looks could kill, I would not have lived to tell about it. "I have to go now," she said. She flagged the waiter down to bring her the bill, and she was 'off like a prom dress'.

What I said to her might seem harsh and cold, but it was the truth. I believe in telling people the truth and anyone who coaches with me is always going to get honesty. If my coaches had not told me the truth about myself, I would not have had the success I have in my life. I make it a point to speak the truth and nothing but the truth. You know why? Because I was once the girl who played all the same kinds of game you play. In a single breath, I could give you all the reasons why it was not possible for me to accomplish a goal. I had all the same conversations in my head that she had in hers. I was the girl who played the ego game like a champion. "I can't leave my family. It's too hard. My mother needs me because she doesn't speak English."

But the little girl became a woman and was still having the same conversations. Remember, the ego resists change. It loves the status quo. These conversations did not help me create freedom, joy, and abundance in my life. Instead, they robbed me of my power to create the very things I desired.

Every time you make excuses about why you can't do something, you are playing the ego game. Every time you decide it's too expensive to hire a coach to guide you through the major life challenges you are facing, you are playing your ego game. Every time you decide not to make time to work on your dreams, you are playing your ego game.

Why am I telling you to stop playing your ego game and start playing the money game? There are several reasons.

Reason #1: *When you play the money game, you learn the rules.* The only way to create massive wealth is to learn the money game. If you don't learn the money game, you cannot produce abundance in your life.

I meet women every day who tell me how they would love to travel with their children, and retire with their husbands. The first question I ask them is, "Do you have a financial advisor?" I nearly always get a blank stare before they say no. I'm good at reading people; what they really want to say is, "A financial advisor is for the rich folks."

My next question is, "Do you have a CPA?" I get the same blank stare before they say no again. At this point, there's an uncomfortable silence between us. And I'm doing my best not to say, "How the heck are you going to retire with your husband and travel the world with your children?"

"A CPA? As in Certified Public Accountant?" As if that's the first time she ever heard the term. "No, I don't have one of those either. I don't have enough money for that to matter."

My last and final question is, "Do you have a budget?"

"Budget? Girl, what's that?"

By the time I get to question number three, I know I'm talking to someone who's playing their ego game and not the money game. These women start telling me how bad they are with money. How they don't budget and their husbands don't budget, but he wants to retire too. Someday.

You want to retire? Stop playing your ego game with money and play the money game for real. If you don't know how to do it, hire the people who know how to play the money game and let them teach you. If you are struggling in your marriage to create freedom, joy, and abundance, and you and your spouse are clueless about finances, hire someone who can help you. If you are living paycheck to paycheck with either nothing left over, or in debt, you need help.

I can teach and support any woman who wants to create abundance in her life, regardless of whether they are single or married. I've created abundance when I was single and also during my marriage. I can hear the conversations in your head:

"Naomi, I don't think I can afford you."

That's fine, but then don't wish and want things you are not willing to work for.

Reason #2: *When you play the money game, you have skin in the game.* Having this powerful woman as my business coach is one thing, but every time she gives me homework I make sure I get it done because her monthly fees are double my California mortgage payment. When you have skin in the game, you do the work. When you don't have stake in it, you slack off and the excuses get fancy and frequent.

Going back to the accountant and financial advisor: Do you think you will handle your money better if you have someone that you know is watching your every penny, or if you can be sneaky and spend money on new shoes if no one's watching? I know for a fact you will be more careful if you're being watched like a hawk. It's human nature.

When I was promoting The Self-Love Summit (I hope you participated and learned a lot!), I sent my Virtual Assistant an email requesting she help me with a PowerPoint presentation for my group coaching program. I told her my business coach wanted me to create a six-month and a year-long program.

Her response was, "Naomi, programs take months to create, and you are in the middle of a summit launch. Don't you think her expectations are unrealistic?"

My answer was, "No!" In fact, I did not care how crazy my coach's expectations were, I was going to deliver because I'm paying her such a high fee. When I think about how my monthly fee can feed my entire village in Haiti, I got moving and I got it done regardless of how hard it was. Bottom line: I got it done!

Reason #3: *You will never win.* I don't care who you are or how much knowledge you have, until you stop playing your ego game and play the money game, you will never win. If you are interested in the money game, you must stop playing around or you will never reach your financial goals. If you want to succeed, then hire someone who's a master at the game you want to play and let them teach you the rules of the game.

What price are you paying for playing your ego game? The cost is not always obvious, but when you play your ego game, you lose the opportunity to create the life you desire. You lose the opportunity to make a difference in the world. You lose the opportunity to be the author of your own story. Instead, you become a victim with a dream.

T. Harv Eker said, "You can be a victim or you can be rich, but you can't be both." Think of it this way: if someone was holding a gun to the head of someone you love, and they told you to take an action or they will kill your loved one, what's the first step you'd take?

Yes, it's that serious. Yes, it's that critical. No, your first step shouldn't be "I think I'll take a wait and see attitude." Like your love one in the above example, your dreams will die. Play the money game, and play it to win!

Chapter 8
Live from a Place of Choice

It's no secret that there's an unequal distribution of wealth in America. Prior to [then] President Barack Obama's State of the Union Address in 2014, the media reported that the wealthiest one percent possess forty percent of the nation's wealth; the bottom eighty percent, own seven percent of the wealth. According to the *Wealth Inequality Report,* the average employee "...needs to work more than a month to earn what the CEO earns in one hour."

Currently, in today's society, there are even more people complaining about the unequal distribution of wealth. Humanity as a whole has fallen into the mindset that there's not enough wealth to go around. People think there's a static pie that never changes or grows; it stays the same so if some people are getting a bigger slice, that leaves less for the others.

But remember, in a free society, there is no one handing out the money. No one dividing it up. Everyone is free to choose: wealth, poverty, or something in between.

In his book *The Science of Being Rich*, Wallace D. Wattle cautions his students about thinking that supply is limited. We live in an abundant universe. Wealth is there for everyone who seeks after it. "Seek and ye shall find." "Knock and the door shall be open to you." You have to seek abundance in order to live an abundant life. Not only is the pie constantly growing, there's more than one pie! The economy is not static; it changes.

Since we are all created equal, it means God has given the poor and the wealthy the exact same faculties. We all get twenty-four hours of the day; no more, no less. The household I grew up in and the churches I attended as a child taught a different concept. My religious tribal family taught me to believe that my riches were in Heaven. I guess when I took on this human incarnation, I forgot to bring them with me. Bummer! The truth completely eluded my consciousness. I grew up asking a lot of questions about wealthy people. Are they different from me? What is that special thing that God gave them and did not give to me? How come some people are able to have plenty of money, while others struggle? How come some people can eat whatever they want, when they want, and never go hungry? How do they go on vacations where and when ever they want?

My mother often told me that Heaven was not for the rich, but for the poor. You see, according to my family, it was a good thing to be poor. It was a good thing to struggle and live paycheck to paycheck. It was good because someday I was going to die and go to Heaven, where I would find my riches exactly where I left them.

Even as a child, I could not buy this. Why would God want his people to suffer and struggle, and only be rewarded when they were dead? I wanted to know the truth about successful people. What made them so special? In my quest for answers, I discovered a simple truth that had eluded me (it also eludes the masses). The truth is, those who create abundance in their lives have lived from a place of choice. And the rest of the people live their lives unconsciously, not choosing, but settling for the default setting of "neutral". These folks are like manufactured robots who have been given a job to do. They never stop and question whether there could be an easier way to carry out the same task.

The people who find it difficult to create abundance in their lives, have yet to tap into the energy that lives within them. They have yet to understand this source of power from which all things are created. The people who find it difficult to be happy here on this planet, don't understand that ultimately you are responsible for your own joy. It is your duty and obligation to find out what they are, and do the things that make you happy.

But how can you do that when you live your life unconsciously? How can you find joy when you're stuck in a career your family chose for you? You chose to become a doctor because everyone in your family is a medical doctor and boy you want to be the one that carries the torch. And you are going to pass the torch on to your children and they will pass it on to their grandchildren. Family traditions like that are functional straightjackets! They encase you in cement and your dreams float around your head, taunting you.

It's time for you to wake up to the fact that you are not living the life you were meant to live. You are living the life your parents (spouse, pastor, girlfriend, boyfriend...you name it) want you to live. You are living the life society says you should live. Parents are wonderful (and they mean well) but sometimes they impede us in our growth toward becoming who we were meant to be. They so desperately want you to do the things they did not do, that they put you in a chute as a small child and shoot you toward *their dreams*. Your parents want you to live the dream they did not have the opportunity to live. The same crazy dream gets passed down from one generation to the next. I'm convinced that this is why panic attacks and anxiety are such major problems in our world today. You are simply not living your truth. You are trying to survive in a straightjacket. To find love, peace, joy, freedom, and abundance you have to find your own (much more comfortable) jacket and wear it proudly.

Here's what happened to me: It's a clear morning. The sun is shining and I awoke to the sound of birds singing. It felt as if I was still in a dream. It was unusual to wake up to the sound of singing birds in Little Haiti. I was disoriented as to where I was and how I'd gotten there. What happened? Had I escaped all the challenges I was facing at such difficult time in my life?

I looked around and saw that I was in the most luxurious room I'd ever seen. Everything was two to three classes above my standard of living. Next to the night stand was a pen with a small pad of paper. It was one of those fancy pens used by sophisticated businessmen. I picked up the pen and it had the hotel name on it. I opened a beautiful black leather folder and saw flyers with the headline of things to do in Clearwater, Florida.

It felt as if I had left my body and traveled to another planet. It took a few minutes for me to remember that I had driven myself there the evening before. I had finally saved enough money to continue with my investigation into the lives of the those who have wealth. The folks I once called 'the rich people'. What did they do differently? I was eager to get to the beach and sit and observe; perhaps I would discover their secrets.

I threw on my blue Daisy Duke shorts, my white tank-top, and a sunhat to complete the outfit. I ran down the hallway and bumped into an older gentleman.

"Good Morning, ma'am," he said. "Are you from around here?"

It was obvious I wasn't a local. My complexion was an instant giveaway. I had also never been referred to as ma'am. I'm from the 'hood and no one spoke like that. He had a heavy Southern accent.

"No sir," I replied, remembering my long unused manners.

"I figured as much," he said, smiling. "What brought you here?"

Before I could open my mouth to say anything, he asked me where I was from.
I said, "I'm not sure."

"You are not an American, are you?" he said.

The moment I had opened my mouth he knew I wasn't a native-born American. Having an accent bothered me because it often meant having a conversation, even when I was not in the mood. Like right then.

"Sir, I don't mean to be rude, but I have to go."

At the beach, I made it a point to speak with the people. They seemed to be very happy and the majority of the people I spoke with were all visiting from different parts of the country. Clearwater is "the place" for beach lovers. Its white sandy beaches and calm surf are known for their beauty.

As I sat watching the seagulls whirl overhead, I could not get the old man out of my mind. I wondered why he was so curious about me. Then a voice in my head told me, "You can choose to slow down."

By sunset I had received the answer to my question: It was a matter of choice. The universe placed that old man there to remind me that I could choose. I had a choice to be in a hurry. I had a choice to slow down. I had a choice to have money, or to be broke. I had a choice to finish college, despite the fact that I had been homeless just three short months prior to my arrival in Clearwater. It was in that moment, I made yet another choice. I chose not to let my situation define me. I chose not to let the color of my skin keep me from breaking bread with those who were different from me. I chose to allow those who know the way, help me find my way.

Too often, people go through life thinking life is something that *happens* to them. Life does not happen to you! You create your life. If you don't have what it is that you desire, or if you are not living the life of your dreams, it's because you are not living from a place of choice. The universe grants us freedom of choice. We each have our own free will. Whether you realize it or not, every minute of the day you are choosing. You are either choosing consciously or you're choosing unconsciously. Either way, you are choosing. If you are not choosing consciously, someone else is choosing for you. That might be your family, friends, or society as a whole (peer pressure). Without making a conscious choice to create what you desire in your life, there will never be any transformation. If you want to create freedom, joy, and abundance in your life, you must first transform the relationship you have with yourself.

How do you live from a place of choice? You make a decision to become conscious of your finances. For example, if I ask you, "What did you spend your last pay check on," and you can't list every dime, you are not conscious of your finances.

You must decide to become conscious about your health. Make a decision to become aware of your thinking. Make a decision to let go of all the excuses you make for why you can't have what you desire. Live from a place of choice. Because if you don't choose, the universe will choose for you.

Before leaving my profession as a Registered Nurse, I had become somewhat complacent. I spent many years complaining about the nursing profession. Though my nursing career opened many doors for me, I always felt I was meant to do something else. But what was it? I had completely forgotten the truth I learned in Clearwater. It's funny how sometimes we have discovered the truth, but it wasn't convenient so we put it away.

Perhaps I put that truth away in my 'someday' box because I was too afraid of the greatness that's within me. Nothing seemed to move for me. The more I complained, the harder it became for me to work as a nurse. I felt like all the other nurses felt: Nursing had become a lucrative career, especially in California where it was easy to make a six-figure income. I was aggressive and good at what I did, therefore, I brought my service to the highest bidder. Traveling around the country, working, going on vacations, and bitching on the job; not a bad life for the little Haitian girl who got teased and bullied for wearing the same dirty pink shorts to school everyday.

The complaining never stopped, but one day I got tired of the complaints. I have a habit of getting tired of the same old stuff. I woke up one day and decided to go for a long hike. It was a perfect California day. I reflected on my life, the trip to Clearwater, Florida, and all the wonderful places I was blessed to have traveled. It was on this hike that I was awakened to the fact that I had fallen off my game. I was doing what average folks do. I was complaining about my life but no one had the power to change it for me. Only I could change it. Only I could create the life I wanted.

After reflecting on the matter, I hired my business coach, Kevin Waldron of Waldron Leadership. During our first meeting, Kevin said something to me that changed the course of my life. He said: "At anytime if you decide to not play the game you were playing, all you have to do is go over to the other side of the fence and play the game you want to play."

Wow! Right there and then I chose to play a different game and I became committed to learning the rules of the new game.

Whatever game you are playing in life, it's the game you chose to play. I was playing a game I no longer wished to play. I knew I was done playing that game but any time I talked about leaving, other people in my immediate environment projected their fears onto me. I decided to stop allowing their fears to rule over me.

You too can choose to play a different game at any time. Everything starts with a conscious decision. The conscious decisions you make are what place you in alignment with whatever it is you desire. You get to decide if you're going to spend the rest of your life alone. You get to decide if you are going to hide in ordinary camouflage for the rest of your life because you are too afraid to walk your bold path. It doesn't matter what the story is; you are the one choosing.

I urge you to live your life according to your own free will and not according to the choices your family makes for you. Living from a place where you are making your own choices keeps you from living with regret, resentment, and anger. If you truly want to be happy, you must not care what anyone thinks of you. Pick up your cross and walk your path. Why is it important to live from a place of choice? Making your own choices about the things you do is very important because it gives your life meaning. Making conscious choices about what you want and desire in your life helps you become more in charge of your life.

When you're in charge of your life, you become happy, and you can now be who you want to be instead of who you think you must to be. It's all up to you. Choose today to be the best, highest you possible!

Chapter 9
Focused Intention

By the time I was thirty-one years old, I had gotten everything I wanted in life. My dream to leave Little Haiti was no longer a dream; it was a reality. My dream to be able to pay my bills effortlessly was also a reality. My desire to travel around the country and explore the East Coast and the West Coast was a reality. I no longer looked at the Golden Gate Bridge on television and hoped one day I would see it. By the time I was thirty-one, I was living six miles from the Golden Gate Bridge and running across the bridge four times a week. I had already manifested the romantic partnership I desired. I was no longer the little girl who told the grand story about the life she was going to live; I had it all.

I had spent several years working on my issues. You can't go through the hell I've been through without accumulating baggage along the way. I had started the process of unwrapping some of those pretty "issues" packages I held on to so dearly. You know, the ones that are so dear to your heart you just can't imagine giving them up. Like my anger. Oh, how I loved my anger: I was angry for my incarnation into a family that I felt didn't love and honor who I was. I was wrong about that, by the way. We can only give what we possess, and what my mother gave me was what she owned. The love and attention I desired from my mother was not what she possessed. She didn't have it to give. My mother knew nothing about love. She'd lost both of her parents by the time she was seven years old. The trauma of losing her mother at that tender age, and having to live in the house with the dead body for two weeks, left her traumatized. The trauma of her sister drowning during her travels to America left her numb and detached. Her husband (my father) and his criminal mind and way of being did not help her situation.

But instead of concentrating on what she failed to give me, I've come to a greater understanding: My mother is a great teacher from the other side. I took my incarnation in the family I did because of the lessons my soul needed for this journey. I would not be who I am today if it had not been for her. I love and admire the person she is because I'm the mirror of my mother. You must embrace what you see in the mirror!

My journey into self-love started after everything on my little wish list had a check mark next to it. I was beginning to look in the mirror and I started embracing all the imperfections the mirror revealed to me. At this point in my life, I had been working with a shrink to help me deal with the past traumas of my life; however, things were not getting better. I was tired of going into his small office, sitting on his couch, and him sitting in front of me like a perfect human being with no challenges in his life. We spent a lot of time discussing my past, and one day I decided to ask him how to get the monkey off my back.

He said, "I don't know how you do that."

Then what am I paying you for?, I thought. In that very moment, it became clear to me that this man could not help me. I was ready to make good with the past and create a new future.

You can't sit around complaining about your past, what others did to you or didn't do for you. You can't sit around not owning your greatness. Going to see a shrink was my way of rejecting what I saw in the mirror. Perhaps he saw something different. My weekly visit to his office allowed me to stay in the past; in order to create a new future and find a new dream, I had to make good with the past.

I begin to look elsewhere for answers, and I read lots of self-help books. A year later, I attended my first seminar with T. Harv Eker, author of *Secrets of the Millionaire Mind*. That's where it all started for me. After the seminar, I was hooked. My soul wanted every single drop of information on how to become a better me.

After studying with every religious denomination known to mankind, I finally found my own religion. It was the religion of becoming a light unto the world. It was the religion of finding the good in me and using it for the good of mankind. My sleeping soul had awakened to something that was bigger than me. For the first time in my life, I understood the meaning of the song "This little light of mine, I'm gonna let it shine." And that's what I do.

A year later, I attended Business Gorilla school with T. Harv Eker. Throughout his teaching, he kept bringing up the word 'intention': "What's your intention?" That was his constant question to his students. I had never heard the word before. I was confused. What's my intention? Heck, I had no idea.

During a morning break, I met a beautiful black woman who was a survivor of the 9-11 attacks. She asked me if I had seen the movie *The Secret* by Rhonda Byron. When I shook my head no, she told me to get the movie and watch it. The following week, after I got home, I brought the movie and I watched it. The movie gave me an understanding about how I had created the life I was currently living. I was hooked on the principles of the universe and how to use universal energy to create the life I desired. Not only was I hooked, but I became an infomercial for the movie. I told everyone who would listen.

However, after watching the movie about a hundred times, I began to see a big piece of the formula was missing. In Rhonda Byron's defense, I have to say I understand why this piece was not in the movie. No one can explain or teach all the principles of the universe in a fifty-minute movie. *Intention was* the missing piece of the puzzle for so many people to whom I recommend the movie. They all said the same thing to me: "Naomi, it doesn't work." I went back and I studied the movie and I realized 'intention' was never covered in the movie.

I'm going to dedicate time here to talk to you about intention. If you follow my instructions, there will be no struggle to create what you desire in your life. Unless you understand intention and how to use it, you will never be able to create or manifest what you desire. I like to stay away from the word 'manifestation' as much as possible and use the word 'create' because I don't want you to think if you visualize it and you give thanks for it, it's going to just show up. That's called daydreaming. It doesn't work that way. You need to have a clear understanding of the process of creation and it starts with FOCUSED INTENTION!

What is intention and why is it so important that you understand it? According to the definition found on Google, intention is having a goal or determination to achieve something. Intention is important because it gives you direction as to what you should do or not do. If you don't set your intention, you will either lose your direction or you won't have any direction at all. Focused intention on the other hand requires that you put all of your energy on what it is you want to create.

The creation process is both simple and complex. I meet women every single day who want to lose weight, find a meaningful relationship, and have the freedom and abundance to travel and do the things that are important to them. For some reason, they have tried every diet and still can't seem to lose the weight, while best friend Jenny dropped forty pounds using the same diet. The problem is, they don't have focused intention. They have a 'want' or a vague desire, but they aren't focused.

If you are trying to launch a new business, get married, and lose twenty pounds all at the same time, you might not be able to make any of it happen. If you do manage to make it happen, you will be so exhausted you don't want to do it again. You have to choose an area you want to work on. If it's your finances, focus on that. If you want to get out of debt and lose twenty pounds, choose one.

Think of each area of your life like a slice of pie. Your finances are a slice. Your health is another slice. Family, career, and community each represent a slice of the pie. When you look at all the areas of your life, which area needs the most work? I can hear you saying "all of them." And it's great to acknowledge that every single area of your life needs work, but to succeed, you must prioritize. Think of the difference between an arrow aimed at a bullseye, and a scatter shot of tiny pellets, spread out over a wide area. Which is more effective? I'm saying it's the arrow. Decide on your target and send a straight, focused arrow toward that bullseye. The scatter shot is going to ping a dozen objects and slay none of them.

So which target is most pressing for you? Is it your health or your finances? Whatever is most pressing for you, that's what you choose. Focus all your energy on that slice of the pie until you get the results you desire. Once you get the results you desire, you can move to the next area (slice of pie) of your life. And the area you spent the last year working on will now only require you to maintain it. For example, if you lost the forty pounds last this year, next year all you need to do is fuel your body with the right food and workout three to four times a week.

I remember the first time I read Napoleon Hill's book *Think Rich and Grow Rich,* I did not understand a single concept in the book. "Where's the part where you get rich," I asked. Years later, I read the book again and realized he gave his readers all the concepts needed to create massive wealth in their lives.

Intention is the seed you plant in the soil of the universe. The seed is your desire, or your wish list. Do you want a lot of money? Do you want to own your own business? Do you want to have the freedom to travel the world? Do you want to find that special person with whom to share your life? What do you want and why do you want it? Your reason behind the want is more important than the want. Your reason for what you want is the intention. This is the seed that you are going to plant into the soil of the universe.

Before I go any further, I want you to get a clear understanding that there is a universal energy; a universal power exists, and whether you believe it exists doesn't really matter; however, this energy is out there. The people who have created massive amounts of wealth do so by entering their co-creation with this energy. The universe is the creator and you are the co-creator. Don't get hung up on religious theory. You can call this energy whatever you want. I call it God. Some of the successful people I work with call it the universe. Whatever you choose to call it doesn't matter, as long as you understand the energy is the creator and you are the co-creator. Your goal is to become a partner (co-creator) with this energy force.

Whatever it is that you want, evaluate your reason for wanting it. If your intention (your reason) for wanting what you want comes from a place of lack and fear, then the seed becomes defective. If the seed is defective, it doesn't matter how much you nurture it, it will never grow and bear fruit.

How exactly do you plant your seed (intention) in the soil of the universe? Once you plant the seed, how do you get it grow or manifest? It's a three-step process.

Step One: *Your intention must be clear.* This means you have to know exactly what you want. You can't guess, you can't wake up today and think it's this and then tomorrow you change it to something else. For example, I was one-thousand percent sure I did not want a life in Little Haiti. You have to know beyond a shadow of doubt that you want a romantic relationship. You have to know you want to do work that you love and enjoy and make a fortune doing it. You better *know* or it will never manifest. You must have crystal clear intentions.

Why is it so important for you to have crystal clear intentions? Michael Beckwith says it this way: "Set the direction and the universe will set the correction." Intentions that are crystal clear help you set the direction where you want to go. This means if you take a wrong step, the universe will guide and place you on the correct path.

I can already hear your self-sabotage mindset. "But Naomi, I don't know what I want?" I disagree. We always know what we want. Your ego is good at making you think you don't know what you want *because not knowing keeps you in limbo*. You cannot create what you want when you're in limbo. If you don't know, do the work necessary to figure it out. You wouldn't be reading this if you didn't, on some level, know what you want. Keeping your desires secret, not telling anyone, not focusing all your attention on it, is the ego's way of keeping you quiet and in the status quo.

You might have trouble becoming clear on your intention. How do you become clear on your intention? You start by visualizing the intention. You paint a clear picture in your mind of what you want. It has to be so clear that you can feel it, smell it, and taste it. You have to see it in your mind's eye. If you can't see it, you can't create it. If you can't imagine yourself with that special person, then you won't ever find the perfect partner. Visualization is hard work. Sports stars learn to visualize themselves winning. They can actually close their eyes and see themselves flying over the defensive line in football, hitting a homerun in baseball, or leaping like a gazelle in ballet. Visualization works.

Many people cannot create what they desire because they are not willing to sit and visualize what they want. Carve ten to fifteen minutes out of your day to sit and think about what you want. Can you see yourself in the beautiful home you desire to own? Can you see yourself as the CEO of the business you want to create? Can you see yourself with that special someone?

After my divorce, I spent several years by myself, being single. Most of my friends at the time thought I was crazy for not at least dating. But I wanted to be crystal clear on what I wanted in a relationship before dating. After a lot of soul searching, I decided I wanted to be in a relationship that allowed me to keep my own identity. I wanted to be with someone who would not attempt to keep me from reaching my highest potential. What I really wanted wasn't a marriage, it had to be a partnership which is different from a lot of marriages. Society teaches us that once you get married you become one with the other person. The Bible even says it. I disagree with this way of thinking because we are not one. You and the person you are with are two separate beings. If you are looking to create freedom, joy, and abundance in your life, it's important for you to understand that you and your significant other are two separate individuals. Your desires will be different and your needs will be different. You may want abundance and he may be content with the situation he is in. In my personal and professional experience, I believe this is one of the major reasons women lose their identity in romantic relationships. Thinking that you are one, you start doing everything your spouse desires and what your children desire and before you know it you are last on the list. You need to change this mindset if you are going to create freedom, joy, and abundance in your life.

After thinking the relationship matter over, I was crystal clear on the fact that I wanted someone with whom I could share my life. I hired a relationship coach to help me with the creation process. We did a lot of work around my intention. I did a lot of journaling about why I wanted a relationship. I loved the journaling part. But then she made me do an exercise that was very uncomfortable. She made me live it even though it wasn't there yet. My nostrils flared, both of my fists were balled up by the end of our session. My coach wanted me to have a romantic dinner where I would pretend this special person was coming over to my house.

"Really, are you out of your mind?" I asked her.

She looked at me and in a calm voice said,

"Do you want a relationship or not?"

"Yes," I said.

"So, you'll prepare the dinner."

I honestly wanted to die. I thought this was such a dumb idea. You see, I skipped the entire part of life where you played make believe as a child. I didn't know how to play make believe. But what I did know was I wanted to meet 'him'.

I went ahead and prepared the romantic dinner for two. I bought a bottle of champagne, and I poured champagne into the empty class next to me. I put food on the empty plate next to me. I talked to him as if he were there. I told him how I felt and the life I wanted to live.

Trust me, it was one of the most uncomfortable things I've ever done, but if you want what you want bad enough, you'll do the work necessary to have it. Thirty days after doing this exercise, I met my husband.

Step Two: *Believe it and live it.* It's not enough to know what you want. You have to believe it and you have to start living as if it has already happened. Go and visit the new house that you want. Drive through the neighborhood during the day. Drive there at night. Find a park in the neighborhood and go sit in the park. After all, you live in the neighborhood. It's natural for you to be in the park. Be comfortable there. Spend time where you want to live. If it's another state, take a vacation there. Remember how I walked through the neighborhood I aspired to live in? Well, now I live in a neighborhood that is even more upscale. Pretend you already have what you want to have. Save money and rent the car you want and drive for a day. Dress like the CEO of the business you want to own. If your desire is a promotion at work, dress for the job you *want,* not the one you have.

Pretend your Mr. Right is already here. Have an intimate conversation with him. Go out on that special date and pretend he is there with you. The truth is, he is. He does exist, you just haven't met him. Everything exists on the spiritual plane first. Everything that exists on Earth was first conceived in the mind! It has to exist in your mind *first* before it can show up in your physical world. Intention alone will not lead to manifestation or creation.

Once your intention is clear, you know *why* you want *what* you want. Make sure your desires are not coming from selfishness, "I want to prove to them they are wrong about me. I'll show them that I'm not the loser they think I am." Remember, you are not doing anything for anyone else. This is not about the other person. It's about you and what you want out of life. As long as you are certain you want something out of self love, you are ready to plant your seed in the soil of the universe.

There's a religious saying my tribal family had: "Prayer changes everything." I disagree. Prayer changes nothing. What changes everything is your ability to enter the co-creation process with God, the universe, or whatever you chose to call it. If prayer changed everything, Haiti would be one of the wealthiest island nations on Earth. The Haitian folks can do some serious praying. My mother prayed a lot, and bless her heart, she is still praying, but nothing has changed for her. It's not about your long, convoluted prayer. It's about planting seeds so you can harvest during the harvest season. Only those who plant seeds get to harvest. You can pray about harvesting all you want to, but if you're not planting seeds, you are not going to have anything to harvest!

Once you have planted your seed in the soil of the universe, there is an incubation period. This means it's going to take time for the seed you planted to grow. It doesn't happen instantly, or overnight. But it does happen.

During the incubation period, one of two things will happen. Either the idea will continue to grow in your mind's eye, or it will die. If the idea doesn't die, then the desire becomes stronger. The stronger the desire, the more you feel the urge to take action. You can't get rid of the idea. You think about it day in night. You might even get up and start reading a blog on relationships. You feel the urgent need to take action. Sometimes the thought of what you want will be very scary. But you can't get rid of it. There is a danger: Your intention can stay in the incubation period forever if you're not careful.

Most people who are having trouble creating what they desire is because their intention is in the incubation period and they can't move on. To get out of the incubation period, you have to re-evaluate your intention. You want to make sure the seed you planted is not defective. You go back to asking the deeper questions.

"What's my real reason for wanting a partnership?"

"What's my reason for wanting freedom, joy, and abundance?"

Make sure that your desires are not coming from a place of fear and lack. If you discover your desire doe not come from a place of love, no worries...just start the process over again. Plant a new seed.

When does your intention leave the incubation period? Once the fear around what you want is gone. Once you let go of needing it. Once you don't feel you need to have it and you've made peace with that. That's when the seed turns into a plant and the plant is what will ultimately bear fruit.

Step Three: *Watering the seed.* What happens if you plant a seed in the ground and you don't water it? Naturally, it withers and dies. It works the same way with your intention. Most people plant their intention in the soil of the universe and nothing comes of it because they fail to water (nourish) their intention.

My husband is a gardener. The man has a green thumb and he can grow just about anything. He grows most the vegetables we eat. He loves to garden and I love to cook. Talk about a match made in heaven! He is very passionate about his garden. I watch him get up first thing in the morning and before he drinks his coffee he goes outside and checks on the seeds or starter plants (sprouts). His very particular about how they should be watered and how much water they should receive. He watches the weather channel and if it's going to be too windy he covers the plants to protect them. One day he wanted to go backpacking. He asked me if I could take care of the garden while he was away for three days.

"Of course, I can," I said. After all, what's so hard about taking care of a garden? You just water a couple of plants and call it a day. Well, it turned out I was wrong. The garden had to be watered at a particular time of the day. Each plant needed a specific amount of water. I completely ignored his instructions and just watered the garden whenever I remembered.

By the time my husband got back, a lot of the starter plants had died. He never said anything to me, but I noticed that he installed an automatic watering system for the garden. He then said to me, "Honey, you won't ever have to water the garden again."

It was then that I understood: The seeds I was planting in the universe needed the same care and attention. Some of the seeds I planted I over-watered because I wanted it so badly. I could not let go of the feeling of "I need to have this" or "I need to make this happen" or the world is going to end.

Speaking of growing life from seeds, we wanted to have a baby. And we were having a hell of a time getting pregnant. As I thought about my husband's garden and how I had over-watered his seeds, I understood why five years later we still did not have the baby we desired. I wanted it too badly. I was frantic and trying to hard. So, I went back, replanted the seed from a place of love, and six months later I was pregnant. Now I'm the mother of a beautiful little soul.

My son is the product of understanding the concept of creation. Did I say all the verbal prayers I was taught growing up? Of course I did, but what I learned was that God doesn't care about how much protesting I do. All he cares about is the root of my desires. I believe and trust that it's going to happen. This is how you put your request into the universe. This is the process I have used over and over again to create the life I have. When the things I desire in my life are not showing up, then I know it's never

God…it's me. I have to go back into the garden and re-water the struggling seedlings, or start over and replant the seeds of my desires.

Like a farmer looking over his fields, let's take a moment to review our own gardens:

What seeds have you planted in the soil of the universe that have yet to bear fruit?

What do you want to show up in your life that is not yet there?

Have you over-watered your desires with fear?

Is it possible you planted seeds that were defective from the start?
Or perhaps you planted no seeds at all, yet expected the blessings of fruit?

Could it be that you have been praying endlessly without ever planting anything in the garden of the universe, and year after year there's nothing for you to harvest?

If the things you want to show up in your

life aren't yet on your doorstep, it's not because the Law of Attraction doesn't work. It's because you have yet to become a master gardener. Look at your desires and ask the deeper questions. Visualize your desires as if they've already happened. Live out your desires by doing one or two simple things that make you feel like you are living your dreams.

And finally, take care of your garden. Water it, but don't over-water it. Pull out the weeds that are choking the seeds you planted. This means getting rid of the beliefs that no longer serve you. Get rid of the people who judge and criticize you. You can still love them, but you don't have to be in their space. Love them from a distance.

Take a stand for yourself and for the things that are important to you.

Chapter 10
Embrace The Mirror

We began with a look in the mirror and talked about YOU being the common denominator in all the problems of your life.

And now as we conclude our journey to a life of freedom, joy, and abundance, we return to the mirror. This time we will embrace what we see there.

Do you understand what I mean when I say that? It's the title of this book: *Embrace the Mirror*. It means many things, such as love yourself, admire your beauty, but also be willing to make changes if you see things that need to be fixed. Embrace it all. It is yours. Own it. Your image in the mirror is a reflection; it's not chiseled in stone. Love your image; you are beautiful. But truthfully, our own flaws (and sometimes our best features) are the hardest for us to see.

I wish someone had told me to look at what was right in front of my face. Sure, I looked at myself in a full-length mirror when I got dressed to go to my high school prom. I looked in the mirror every time I wore a bridesmaid's dress. I spent the first sixteen years of my life looking at myself in the mirror every Sunday as I dressed to go to church, where I listened to the sermons that killed my spirit.

Honestly, when I looked in the mirror I never noticed anything beyond the color of my skin. My flat nose, nappy hair, my bulging thighs and the backside I hid by wearing clothes two sizes too big. I saw only the physical (perceived) flaws. I saw the chalk outline of my body, but I did not see beyond that.

I did not know that I was more then the color of my skin or the shape of my nose. Or that I was bigger and greater then the circumstances that attempted to define me. I never saw in the mirror the invisible tool belt I had been wearing around my waist. Everything I needed for my journey was in that tool belt. The tools were love and compassion for myself and for others. Kindness was there and so was resilience, because God knew I would need that to climb the many mountains I created for myself.

You see, God placed this tool belt around my waist because he knew I would experience disappointment, hunger, anxiety, frustration, heartaches, and loneliness. He knew I would walk the Earth looking for where I belonged. He knew I would become a lost sheep caught in many storms. And so he gave me what I would need to survive. He did not give me the answers to the test, he gave me the tools to ace the test!

Indeed, there is a mirror that sees beyond the color of your skin. You are more than your ethnicity. You are much more than your age or your weight. When I talk about embracing the mirror, I'm asking you to take a hard look at yourself. Go beyond the clothes you are wearing, whether they are designer labels or Walmart 'fashion'. Go beyond the eye shadow, the lipstick, the artificial nails, and the hair extensions. I'm not sure if you wear hair extensions, but I'm a black woman and honestly, I love my hair extensions! They are a part of my look, but they are not me.

Embracing the mirror means seeing beyond your physical body. You are able to see your own dark shadow, the side of you that you won't dare explore because you might just discover your true essence. And I get it – that scares you. It scared me too, at first. You might discover that you are an energy that cannot be destroyed. You might discover you are bigger and greater than the trials in your life. You might discover there is a giant living inside of you and this giant is not afraid of anything or anyone.

Embrace the mirror means to accept the fact that you are a spiritual being who is here to have a human experience in the body you have chosen as your vessel for this journey. It means taking responsibility for the good, the bad, and the ugly. It means accepting your pain, anger, and frustrations. It means loving every aspect of who you are.

Embrace the person you were yesterday, five years ago, or even a decade ago. That was you; good, bad, or indifferent. You can't change what you were. But as a human being, you are constantly evolving and becoming something new and different. You are like a caterpillar clinging to a twig or a leaf. You then spin yourself into a cocoon to become a beautiful butterfly. Five years ago, the stuff you ate as a caterpillar tasted really good, but now your butterfly appetite has changed. The person you married felt right at the time. Today, you wish you had known then what you know now.

Today, you desire someone who can be a better father to your children. You desire someone who can handle his responsibilities like a man. You desire someone who can support you on your journey of creating the life you want to live. Today, you desire to be more than just a mom because you have something burning inside you. You have something…a persistent little voice…telling you to do more and be more. You no longer wish to sit in a cubical or stand at a station carrying out one brainless task after another. You feel you have a message to share with the world. You can't quite explain the loneliness you feel inside, because you know no one gets it. On the outside, it looks like you have everything, but the truth is… you have lost yourself in this journey called life.

You wish you hadn't gained all the weight that came with child bearing. You wish you had not neglected yourself for the sake of family. Whatever your wishes are, I want you to understand that you are a caterpillar always undergoing a transformation every single day of your journey.

There are moments in your life where you will be the beautiful butterfly that everyone looks at and admires. You will look back at old photos of yourself and wonder what happened and how you got to this point. If you can remember this simple concept of transforming from a caterpillar into a butterfly you will always know that you are in a different season of your life. Perhaps now you are in the caterpillar season, and you're just eating upside down from a twig or a leaf. You don't quite know who you are anymore. The path you should take isn't clear to you yet. But I urge you to be patient with yourself. I urge you not to rush the process.

Here's how it happened for me: It was a Friday afternoon. The air was thick with humidity and the smell of sweat. I pulled up to my favorite hole-in-the-wall restaurant. It was housed in a tiny white building with a single square window barely large enough to stick your face into. The building looked like it had been recently pressure-washed and was waiting for a paint job. Cars surrounded the building, as a line of people waited for their number to be called, and that magical moment when you stepped up to the window and got your bag; your own little slice of heaven. The aroma from each person who walked by with their bag had me drooling and my tummy rumbled like a hungry bear coming out of hibernation. Everything on the menu was delicious so it was always hard to choose. I know I'm a little biased, but Haitian food is the best cuisine in the entire Caribbean. Better than Cuban. Better than Jamaican. And much better than the other side of the island, from the Dominican Republic. Again, that's just my opinion. Haitian food is a magical blend of French, Spanish, and many other native flavors. Haitian cooks learn early in life how to use the sea's bounty and the land's offerings.

I ordered my grandmother's favorite foods; legumes and conch, white rice with black bean sauce, a staple of our diet in Haiti. Conch is very much like clams, but it's plentiful in the islands and is used a lot, from deep fried to cold salads. I love it. All around the Caribbean Islands you will see small mountains of pink conch shells, like monuments to the mighty little creatures.

So, once I had my sack of Haitian soul food, I raced to the new house I had purchased for my grandmother, and found her sitting at the kitchen table. The little house had taken its share of use and mistreatment, just like I had. Maybe that's what had attracted me to it; we were both survivors.

The kitchen table was now old and wobbly; I had purchased as a Mother's Day gift ten years earlier. This kitchen table was not a place where we ate or shared our lives. It was a place where my mother and the rest of my siblings stored junk mail, homework, old newspapers, and coupons. The messy table was symbolic of how dysfunctional our lives were. I see that now, but didn't see it then. It was just annoying.

But that day, as I entered with the sack of food, I saw that my grandmother had cleaned up the table! She had removed all the junk mail and litter and put everything in brown paper bags, which she had stacked in the living room. The table had somehow transformed in front of me. It was no longer the disgusting wobbly table I hated. The table now represented the table at my grandmother's house in Haiti where meals were shared and stories were told.

My grandmother, as you will recall, had always had a serious nature about her. She never really smiled much, but when the occasion called for laughter, she would laugh full out, until tears rolled down her face.

She signaled me to sit down as she pulled out a couple of plates for us. On this particular day, I felt like a drifter who had no purpose and was worried about where the next wave would throw me. It was exciting, and unsettling at the same time. Why such a big change? Why had she cleared the table?

We sat down to eat and the aroma from the

food was killing me. I was hungry, so I jammed the food down my throat like someone who had been in a concentration camp. My grandmother put down her fork and stared at me. She could tell something was bothering me.

"Anything you want to tell me?" she asked calmly.

"No, I'm just starving," I said. "Thanks for clearing the table. It's nice."

She looked skeptical but dug her fork into the conch and rice and took a big bite. "It is good," she said. High praise coming from her.

I had a lot I wanted to tell her but I knew I shouldn't share with her the battles I had been having with my mother; the battles that had led to me moving out of the very house I'd purchased. My grandmother had never been a big fan of my mother so it wasn't that I worried about her not being on my side; however, there were other things on my plate.

Once my stomach had been a little bit calmed, I decided to share with her my concern around being the only Haitian girl who graduated high school and college and had yet to find a husband. I proceeded to tell her about my future plans and how I was determined to be more than just a drifter. I poured my heart out to her.

She listened and then looked at me with tears in her eyes. Her hair was white like snow and the deeply etched wrinkles on her face revealed she too had been a drifter, looking for her place in the universe.

"You are a tortoise," she said.

I always wanted to scream when she said cryptic things like that, like we were in some Ralph Macchio movie where *The Karate Kid* is given some mystical advice from Pat Morita. "Grasshopper, you are a tortoise."

I looked at her, puzzled and as usual, because I had no idea what she was talking about. She proceeded to tell me the story of the tortoise and the hare. After telling me the story she said, "It's better to be the tortoise than the hare."

Indeed, of course she was right. My grandmother was nearly always right. She was a very wise woman. She knew that it's better not to rush the process of discovering who you are. You don't have to know what your purpose is or what it is you came here to do. All you need to do right now is to be kind to yourself. Have the same empathy for yourself that you have ready for those who are dying. Show the same kindness to yourself that you show to your children, friends, and relatives. You are exactly where you need to be because there isn't any mistake in the universe.

No matter the season you are in, I want you to embrace the person you are now. I don't care if you lack confidence. Embrace the woman who is searching for who she is and her mission and purpose in this life. Embrace the woman who no longer desires to live her life through the lens of her ex-husband, children, or other women in your lineage. Embrace your currently reality. Because only then will you move to the next season in your life. You have to embrace the person you were yesterday, five years ago, or even a decade ago. As a human being, you are constantly evolving and becoming something new.

I later discovered that there was another mirror screaming at me. The mirror that was screaming at me to accept all my imperfections. The mirror that was screaming at me to stop sacrificing my needs, wants, and desires for the sake of others. The mirror that constantly screamed, "Don't you get who you are?" The mirror that said, "Are you completely clueless about the gifts you possess?"

I never looked in that mirror because no one had ever taught me to look in the mirror of my life. Today, right now, I'm urging you to look in the mirror of your life. What is the mirror saying to you? What do you need to purge and what do you need to keep? Remember, unless you get rid of the old, the new and better cannot enter your life.

Embracing the mirror is really a process and it won't happen overnight. It's a three-step process. Just like the caterpillar undergoes a slow transformation to become a butterfly, you have to undergo a transformational process to become the person you were meant to be.

Step One: *Accept who or what the mirror reveals to you.* No more pretending to be someone or something you are not. No more pretending it doesn't matter when your voice isn't heard. You must stop wearing the hat that doesn't fit you.

My mirror revealed to me that my place in this world is not that of caretaker. Taking on that role had been an unconscious choice I had made. My place in this great big universe is to motivate, teach, and inspire women across the globe, no matter the color of their skin, race, religion, or nationality. My role in this great big universe is to help women embrace their authentic selves so they can create the life they want for themselves and their children. My place in this world is to help you recognize who you are. My place in this world is to help you return to your source of energy. It's my duty to help you come home to yourself.

Step Two: E*mbrace all the things you once were.* Embrace your culture and your ethnicity. Embrace the woman who was once voiceless. Embrace the woman who stayed a bit too long in the relationship that was not working, in the hopes it would someday get better. Embrace the woman who never once consciously planted a single seed in the soil of the universe. The past helped make you who you are at the moment. The butterfly could never skip the cocoon phase. I now embrace the caregiver in me, even though my soul no longer desires to take care of the members of my tribe, or those confined to a hospital bed. The caregiver in me allowed me to pave the way for the women who will be on this journey long after I'm gone. Perhaps a young woman who is going through what I've been through might come across this book and use it to transform her life by applying the principles I teach. If you once neglected yourself, now is not the time for regrets. It's time for you to embrace it and make good with the past and start being the woman who is quite capable of putting herself on the list.

Step Three: *Forgive yourself.* You are on a journey and there are many twists and turns. Until you forgive yourself for who you've been or who you haven't been, you won't be able to grow the wings you need to fly. Until you forgive yourself, you will stay in the cocoon phase of your life. You should forgive yourself. You should love and honor who you are. Everything you've done and experienced until this moment of your life was to prepare you for the freedom, joy, and abundance you are going to create for your self.

Every experience was to expand your consciousness and help you grow wings that can sail above the thunder and lighting you will face on the journey toward the life you desire. Wings that are immature cannot withstand the current of the wind. Forgiveness for yourself will give you the strong wings you need to soar beyond the clouds. There is no need to cry over the cocoon you are in now because the truth is, you are a work in progress, waiting to emerge once again with grace, love, dignity, and purpose.

Now all you need to do is see yourself as part of this great energy. Again, you can call it whatever you desire. Know that you came from the source who is a master of creation. He created this masterpiece—a planet called Earth. He placed all sorts of people on the planet from every walk of life. Choosing to see yourself as part of this energy is a conscious choice. Stop listening to religious sermons telling you that you are less than this energy and that you are at the mercy of this energy. The truth is, you are the same as this energy. Every human being on this planet is a creator in his own right. There's greatness in every single creator on the planet and there is greatness in you. Those who understand this principle go on to create massive amounts of wealth and have success in every single area of their lives.

I have consciously chosen to tap into this energy. I want you to know that there is only one energy that governs the universe. There are, however, two sides to this abundant energy: Light and Dark. Each and every one of us gets to choose what part of the energy we want to plug into. You can plug into the dark side of the energy, or you can plug into the light. The choice is yours. The beautiful thing about this energy is that you can also choose to unplug at anytime. If you were plugged into the dark side of the energy and you no longer desire to be in the dark, you have the right to unplug from the dark and plug into the light. The energy will never judge you for having plugged into the dark side. The only person who ever judges you is you. You are the one who has allowed others' judgments of you to define who you are; however, that is not who you are in the eyes of universe. You can change anytime you choose. Isn't that great news? I am so happy to share that with you!

To create freedom, joy, and abundance in your life, I urge you to plug in to the light side of this energy. Once you do that, you will begin to discover the tools given to you for your journey. Let go of the pain and resentment. Turn them over to this energy. Allow Him to mend your broken dreams. When you are ready to start the journey of creating the life you desire, don't hesitate to reach out to me at www.embracethemirror.com.

I'm your sister on the journey to creating a life rich with freedom, joy, and abundance. Together there is nothing we can't accomplish!

Acknowledgements

The day my husband asked me to marry him, I said, "I will not marry you unless you make a conscious decision to have money. I do not desire to be broke and broken."

He said, "Honey, I don't understand it, but I don't mind having the [financial] freedom to go backpacking."

I want to thank my husband, Robert Sodomin, for joining with me on the journey to freedom, joy, and abundance.

I am forever grateful for David Sodomin, my beautiful son, for inspiring me to be the best version of myself.

Heartfelt thanks and tremendous gratitude to the following Team Naomi members, without whom I could not have achieved my goals:

Diligent editor, Pat Barnhart of Writing Down Pat, who's been on this journey with me from the start. Thank you for creating a safe space where I can nurture and grow my love of writing and helping women succeed.

Business coach, Kevin Waldron from Waldron Leadership, for holding me accountable for my magnificence.

Susie Carder, CEO of Motivating the Masses, for being my friend, teacher, and supporter. This book would not exist if the universe had not brought us together. I love and appreciate the strong, talented, and beautiful being that you are. You are my Earth Angel. I love you.

Katy Kidd, Steve Kidd, and the rest of the Kidd Marketing group for making this book happen. If not for your love of nurturing authors and making sure their message gets into the hands of those who need it, this book would not exist.

Lisa Nichols and her team for creating a community where unicorns such as myself are encouraged to be who we are. I love the valuable work you have done and continue to do.

FREE GIFT!

GET A 30-MINUTE COACHING CALL
WITH THE AUTHOR
($650.00 VALUE!)

To claim your free gift, go to
www.embracethemirror.com and click on
Schedule link to book your free session.

Made in the USA
San Bernardino, CA
28 September 2018